THE BERLIN WALL

THE BERLIN WALL

Division of a City

Thomas Flemming
Documents, Berlin Wall Archives: Hagen Koch

be.bra verlag
berlin.brandenburg

Bibliografische Information
der Deutschen Bibliothek
Die Deutsche Bibliothek verzeichnet diese
Publikation in der Deutschen
Nationalbibliografie; detaillierte
bibliografische Daten sind im Internet über
http://dnb.ddb.de abrufbar.

Aktualisierte Auflage
© be.bra verlag GmbH,
Berlin–Brandenburg, 2006
KulturBrauerei Haus S,
Schönhauser Allee 37, 10435 Berlin
post@bebraverlag.de
Editor: Gabriele Dietz, Berlin
Picture editing: Gabriele Dietz/Th. Flemming
Translation: Penny Croucher, London
The Route of the Wall:
Ditha Ahmadi/Peter Palm, Berlin
Typografie und Umschlag:
Iris Farnschläder, Hamburg
Layout: Daniel Sauthoff, Hamburg
(Cover photo Klaus Lehnartz, Berlin)
Typeset: Excelsior 9 pt and Folio
Lithography: Bildpunkt, Berlin
Druck und Bindearbeiten: Friedrich Pustet, Regensburg
ISBN 3-930863-74-X
ISBN 978-3-930863-74-7

www.bebraverlag.de

Acknowledgements
We are grateful to the following for reprinting
permission:
Basis Druck Berlin for a quote from
"Halt! Grenzgebiet! Leben im Schatten der
Mauer" by Thomas Scholze and Falk Blask;
Brandenburgisches Verlagshaus for passages
from "Ausgegrenzt. Der Fall der DDR-Grenztruppen" by Volker Koop;
Ch. Links Verlag for passages from "Geisterbahnhöfe" by Christoph Links, Heinz Knobloch
and Thomas Wenzel; from "Chronik des Mauerfalls" by Hans-Hermann Hertle;
S. Fischer Verlag for a passage from "Vierzig
Jahre" by Günter de Bruyn
and Klaus Schlesinger for a passage from his
book "Am Ende der Kindheit".

This book is based on Th. Flemming/H. Koch,
"Die Berliner Mauer – Geschichte eines
politischen Bauwerks"
ISBN 978-3-930863-88-4
be.bra verlag, Berlin 2004

Contents

A WALL THROUGH BERLIN

The Border is closed

At 1.11 a.m. the East Berlin radio service interrupted their "Night-time Melodies" for a special announcement:
"The governments of the States of the Warsaw Pact appeal to the parliament and government of the GDR and suggest that they ensure that the subversion against the countries of the Socialist Bloc is effectively barred and a reliable guard is set up around the whole area of West Berlin."

The significance of this pretentious declaration was quite clear: West Berlin was to be sealed off. But in the West, who on earth listened to SED (East German) radio…

It was Sunday 13 August 1961. At 1.05 a.m. the lights suddenly went out at the Brandenburg Gate. Armed GDR border guards and members of combat groups marched up and positioned themselves at the inner city demarcation line. In the glare of the headlights of military vehicles they ripped up the paving stones and erected barbed wire barriers. The scene was the same at many points in and around Berlin: Border Police, armoured vehicles, barbed wire, concrete posts.

At this point the West was completely unaware of the dramatic developments taking place at the sector borders. Chief Superintendent Hermann Beck was preparing himself for routine duty at the headquarters of the West Berlin Police on Tempelhofer Damm; there had been no special incidents since the beginning of the shift at 5.30 p.m. "Person seeking help at Zoo station", "Drunken teenager at Wittenbergplatz". Just the usual sort of thing on a Saturday night in Berlin.

At about 2.00 a.m. a report came in which at first Beck didn't know how to deal with: "13.8.1961, 01.54. Spandau police station report that the S-Bahn train from Staaken

13th August 1961: Members of combat troops form a cordon at the Brandenburg Gate.

travelling to Berlin was directed to return to the Soviet Zone. The passengers had to get out and their fares were refunded." Just one minute later a further call was received from Wedding police station: "At 01.55 S-Bahn trains in both directions were halted at Gesundbrunnen Station." Then further calls followed, one after another; all S-Bahn trains were also stopped at Schönholz, Wannsee and Stahnsdorf stations.

The reports, coming in quick succession from 2.20 a.m. onwards, became increasingly threatening. "15 military trucks with Vopos (East Berlin police) at Oberbaumbrücke". "Armoured reconnaissance vehicles on Sonnenallee". "Hundreds of Vopos and Border Police with machine guns at the Brandenburg Gate." Beck was almost in a state of panic. Was it the attack on Berlin which everyone feared? Should he fetch the sealed envelope from the safe and set in motion the secret plan for the defence of West Berlin which would throw the capital cities of the West into turmoil? For a quarter of an hour Beck and his superior wrestled with a decision which carried serious consequences. When the telephone reports up to

2.45 a.m. continued to speak of "concentrations of troops", and "blockades" but not of "advances on to West Berlin territory", they decided to give the "minor alarm" for the time being.

During the night a total of 13,000 West Berlin police were woken from their sleep and called in. A former police officer commented that "at first we thought they were going to overrun us and march into West Berlin, but they remained precisely within one centimetre inside the sector boundary."[1]

It was an operation planned and executed by the General Staff, which was led by an SED official hardly known in the West, Erich Honecker. The 49 year old General Secretary of the Defence Committee was at the nerve centre of operations throughout the night. He worked from the Police Headquarters at Alexanderplatz where he received reports by telephone and courier on the progress of the blockade measures and issued orders to the Commanders. A total of 10,500 operational units of the Peoples' and Border Police and members of fighting groups were directly involved in sealing off West Berlin that night. In addition there

Armoured vehicles of the GDR People's Police (Volkspolizei) take up position at the Brandenburg Gate.

were several hundred Stasi workers as well as two motorised armoured divisions of the NVA (altogether about 8,000 men) who, however, were ordered to approach the border only as far as 1,000 metres in a "second back-up formation".

Everyone went according to plan. Only 12 of the 81 street crossing points remained passable, the rest were sealed off with barbed wire. The S-Bahn trains running between the two parts of Berlin, as well as into the surrounding area, were stopped. On 23rd August the number of border crossing points was reduced to seven: Friedrichstraße, Bornholmer Straße, Chausseestraße, Invalidenstraße, Heinrich-Heine-Straße, Oberbaumbrücke, Sonnenalleee and Friedrichstraße/Zimmerstraße (Checkpoint Charlie).

Walter Ulbricht had achieved his political aim. The escape route across the Berlin sector border, which had been used over many years by more than 1.6 million East German citizens fleeing into the West, had been blocked. It had taken the SED leader a great deal of effort over the past months and days to convince the Soviet Party and State leader Khrushchev and the other Warsaw pact leaders that sealing off West Berlin was the only way to stop the flood of refugees and prevent the GDR from "bleeding to death".

On 12th August 1961 at about 4 p.m. Ulbricht signed the necessary orders and the operation swung into action.

It wasn't until 12th August when they were instructed by the Minister for Defence, Heinz Hoffmann, that the NVA commanders were brought into the plan. At 8 p.m. an order was issued to them to "support the armed forces of the Ministry for the Interior in securing the Sector borders in and around West Berlin. The troops of the National Volksarmee in the ordered sections,

together with the forces of the 1st and 8th motorised armoured divisions, are to form a second back-up formation at a distance of about 1,000 metres from the border."[2]

During the night the Soviet troops around Berlin were put on alarm level 1, although throughout the whole operation they were not supposed to put in an appearance if at all possible.

During the preparations for closing the borders, Ulbricht and Honecker bypassed almost all the leading organs of the Party and State. Even the leaders of the so-called Block Parties knew nothing on the evening of 12th August when they were invited by Ulbricht to come for a meal at his summer residence in Groß-Dölln, 75 kilometres north of Berlin. It wasn't until about 10 p.m. that the amazed guests were informed that the sector borders with West Berlin were about to be closed.

It was a warm August night after a hot Saturday. At 2.30 a.m. Allan Lightner, the Senior Representative of the US government in Berlin, received the information about the closing of the sector border – and went back to sleep. He was to be woken as soon as there were any further developments. At 3.30 a.m. the CIA employee, John Kenney, heard that the border was closed via a radio announcement on RIAS (Radio in American Sector, ed.). Shortly afterwards, when he walked into the CIA Headquarters in Dahlem, he expected frenzied activity. Yet the whole building was quiet, with no sign of any alert.

Meanwhile Richard Smyser, an employee of the US-Mission, had received the order from the Duty Officer to "take a look round" in Berlin. At 3.30 a.m. he arrived at Potsdamer Platz. He demanded information about what was going on from the Border Police stationed there – and also his right to go across. After a short exchange of words

Geheime Verschlußsache

den 12.8.1961
Ho/Ke.

Kandidat des Politbüros
des ZK der SED
Genosse Gerhard G r ü n e b e r g

P o t s d a m

Geheime Kommandosache
27 (persönlich!) 27

Nr. 24/61
2 Exemplare je 1 Blatt
2' Exemplar 1 Blatt
-221

Werter Genosse Grüneberg!

Ich bitte Dich, entsprechend der getroffenen Vereinba-
rungen am 13. August 1961, ab 01.30 Uhr die erforder-
lichen Maßnahmen zu veranlassen. Die Dir bekannten
Dokumente werde ich Dir im Verlaufe der Nacht über-
mitteln. Den in der Anlage beigefügten Befehl an den
Vorsitzenden der Einsatzleitung Potsdam, Genossen
S e i b t , bitte ich um 01.30 Uhr zu übergeben.
Desweiteren füge ich diesem Schreiben die Entwürfe für
die Alarmbefehle an die Einsatzleitungen der Kreise
Oranienburg, Nauen, Potsdam, Zossen und Königswuster-
hausen bei sowie den Entwurf einer Bekanntmachung des
Rates des Bezirkes Potsdam.

Mit sozialistischem Gruß

E. Honecker

Anlagen

The countdown begins. On 12th August 1961 Honecker sets off the chain of command to close the border.

the barbed wire was indeed pushed aside so that Smyser could drive through in his car. As dawn was breaking on the streets of East Berlin he saw military vehicles, armoured personnel carriers and trucks carrying barbed wire and concrete posts; but he didn't see a single Soviet tank.

In Washington the first news from Berlin arrived shortly after 5 a.m. MEZ (about midnight local time). John Ausland, an employee of the Berlin section of the US Foreign Ministry, was the first to be informed. He listened to the telephone report and then went back to bed. Four hours later he received a CIA telegram from Berlin which contained the code word instructing that the President should be informed immediately. At this point Ausland hurried into the State Department and urgently looked through the documents for the plans for this particular case. After a lengthy search he at last found a file with the corresponding title, "Border Closure". It was empty.

At 12.30 p.m. local time President John F. Kennedy was advised of the situation on board his yacht. At first he was indignant at not having being told about the events in Berlin earlier but quickly calmed down. Together with Secretary of State, Dean Rusk, he put together a press release and then said, "I'm going sailing now. Go to your baseball game as you planned." The press release ran, "It is clear to whole world that sealing off of East Berlin is a defeat for the communist system. The East German Ulbricht regime is responsible for shutting in its own people in front of the eyes of the whole world."

Within his circle of close advisers Kennedy made no secret of his relief about developments. "Khrushchev would not have had a wall built if he really wanted to take West Berlin. If he were to occupy the whole city he wouldn't need a wall … . It's not a par-ticularly pleasant solution but a wall is a damned sight better than a war."[3] Furthermore the "three essentials" of the American policy in Berlin had not been affected: 1. The presence of the Western Allies in Berlin; 2. Free access routes; 3. The right of self-determination for the West Berliners. There was, therefore, little cause for Washington to enter into vigorous negotiations.

In West Berlin, however, things were viewed completely differently on 13th August. The Governing Mayor, Willy Brandt, was not in the city but on a special election campaign train travelling from Nürnberg to Hannover. Brandt was the SPD candidate for Federal Chancellor in the forthcoming general election in September 1961. He was woken up at 4.30 a.m. by Heinrich Albertz, the head of the Berlin Chancellery, and took the first plane back to Berlin. "I was greeted by Albertz and Police President Stumm at Tempelhof Airport. We were driven to Potsdamer Platz and up to the Brandenburg Gate and saw the same scene everywhere: construction workers, obstacles, concrete posts, barbed wire and East German military personnel. At Schöneberg Town Hall I received reports that Soviet tanks were encircling the city on standby and that Walter Ulbricht had already been seen congratulating the units of construction workers … ."[4] During the course of the morning Brandt experienced feelings of rage and fury, but also of concern over a possible escalation of the situation.

It was still morning when Brandt drove out to the leafy suburb of Dahlem to meet with the Allied Commandants. He asked insistently what action the Western Allies had in mind and at first he was met with an embarrassed silence. With mounting anger the Mayor demanded that at least a strong protest should be lodged in Moscow and added, "At the very least send patrols to the border between East and West Berlin to

counter the feelings of insecurity and to show the West Berliners that they are not in any danger!" The three Allied Commandants agreed to this at any rate, but otherwise they could seen no reason for any activity, especially as they were waiting for instructions from their respective capital cities.

A sense of being left in the lurch spread among the population of West Berlin. "The West is doing nothing," ran the headline of the Bild-Zeitung on 16th August and this expressed the feelings of half the city. Faced with this situation Brandt decided on an unusual course of action: circumventing the US Allied Commandant, he sent a telegram to US President Kennedy. Employing a directness which was hardly diplomatic, the Berlin Mayor demanded action from the Western powers. "1. Lack of action and a purely defensive stance could cause a crisis of confidence in the Western powers. 2. Lack of action and a purely defensive stance could lead to over-confidence within the East Berlin regime…"

On the afternoon of 16th August 300,000 West Berliners gathered in front of the Schöneberg Town Hall to demonstrate. The atmosphere was heated. The placards read: "We need protection. Where are the protecting powers?"; "Enough of protests. Now let actions speak"; "Deceived by the West". Brandt was faced with a difficult task. On the one hand he had to address the peoples' feelings but on the other hand he had to prevent a heightening of the situation and any rash action at the barricades.

He struck the right tone in his speech: "The Soviet Union has let their guard-dog Ulbricht off his lead and allowed him to march into the Eastern Sector of this city … The protests of the three Allied Commandants were right but this is not end of the matter!" He appealed urgently to the civil and military leaders of the GDR: "Don't debase yourselves! Show humanity wherever possible and above all, don't shoot at your own people! This city of Berlin wants peace but is not going to capitulate. …"

In the meantime in Washington alarming reports were coming in from Berlin. A State

West Berliners registering their protest with Willy Brandt in front of the Schöneberg Town Hall on 16th August.

Department official telegraphed: "There is a danger that that fragile thing called hope could be destroyed."[5] In this situation Kennedy decided to take two symbolic actions. He sent 1,500 GIs down the motor-way from Helmstedt to strengthen the US garrison in Berlin, where they were given a tumultuous welcome by the population. He also sent his Vice-President Lyndon B. Johnson to the beleaguered city. When John-son arrived at Tempelhof Airport on 19th August he was overwhelmed by the trium-phal reception. Hundreds of thousands of people lined the route of his journey through the Western sectors.

The situation in East Berlin

While pictures of the anger and protests of the West Berliners were flashed round the world, the situation in the Soviet Sector hardly reached the outside world. "Trams and olive-green military trucks were driving past full of uniformed personnel with iron expressions," wrote the author Klaus Schle-singer recalling the events of 13th August

"Everywhere it was the same picture, chains of armed combat groups and on both sides, people. I ... ran instinctively along the streets near the border ... there were people everywhere in front of crumbling façades, shaking their heads and waving their arms about passionately."[6]

The GDR press printed nothing but reports of triumph and messages of solidarity. The "Neue Deutschland" on 14th August ran quotes from "workers of the GDR and its capital" such as: "To Walter Ulbricht young railway workers say: Let's get out of the danger area of West Berlin!" – "We can breathe a sigh of relief" – "Woe betide any-one who gets pushes their luck!" Today, access to the secret reports of the SED dis-trict leaders gives a true insight into the atmosphere among the East Berlin popula-tion immediately after the closing of the border. These "information reports"[7] show a surprisingly unvarnished picture of the reactions within the boroughs. The reports, which were analysed centrally and passed on to Ulbricht, make it clear to the SED

Widening the border strip. Improving the installations at Checkpoint Charlie in November 1961.

leadership exactly what many people in East Berlin really thought of the "anti-fascist protective Wall".

From Wollankstraße in the borough of Pankow at 10.30 a.m. on the morning of 13th August an anonymous informer reported: "A woman screamed out, "Let's go into the middle of the street and force our way through the barrier. We are all Germans, we want to go over to our brothers." Other young people shouted "It's a disgrace that you are prepared to guard this border and not let us across. You are not Germans."

A more subdued report from Weißensee, also made on 13th August runs: "Although relatively scattered, there is a string of open declarations of support," and, "there is a large number of negative statements, which in essence express the following content: – deepening of the rift by us (SED, ed.), – limitation of freedom, – this isn't a democracy, and in a number of the conversations the fear of war is a repeated theme." In the initial stages of criticism the regime took vigorous action in many places: "On Schönhauser Allee Station a troublemaker was arrested who said, among other things: "There is no democracy in this country", and that he would soon find a gap where he could slip through to the other side."

"Near the East Berlin Zoo, on tram number 69E, trouble was stirred up by a BVG employee: "They must be frightened over there, 300 tanks have been brought in and the tracks have been pulled up." When a comrade squared up to him he started begging for bananas for his children and so on …The comrade was told how to deal with such troublemakers in future." On 16th August the "section for organisation and personnel" of the SED District Headquarters in Weißensee reported that: "A Frau Dienzloff,…Weißensee, at a Party meeting of the National Front said: 'Now we are sitting behind barbed wire and they call that freedom.'"

As the "information reports" show, there were many different forms of protest: "In the PKB Kohle a member of the combat group was arrested because he had criticised the Party and the government and had refused to obey orders. At some points there were "coinciding" work breaks, exactly at the same time as the DGB in West Berlin was calling for a so-called protest strike. In the VEB thermal power station the belt on a machine was changed over at that time … with the result that the machines broke down. In the VEB dairy a machine was repaired at 11 a.m. and thereby caused …

November 1961: At Potsdamer Platz the border is reinforced with camouflage nets and tank obstacles.

a shut-down. During the lunch hour on 15th August the following slogan was painted on to the works' wall at OWL, Treptow: "Berlin is now a prison." The perpetrators have not been traced yet."

In these critical days the SED sent several dozen "agitators" on to the street to interfere in discussions and disperse the larger gatherings. They did not have an easy task.

There were individual cases of open disobedience: "Comrade Danis from the Drolhagen brigade has refused to build the sector border. He was isolated from his brigade immediately and later his papers (SED Party book etc.) were taken away from him."

Occasionally, a few policemen and border guards also protested openly and refused to obey orders. For example, on 15th August a police officer did not turn up for duty. "Although during the ensuing discussion he was advised of his politically incorrect behaviour, he reacted by giving up his Party papers and his record of service. The necessary measures were taken." By the end of August, according to an inventory made for Ulbricht in East Berlin alone, 2,192 people were arrested and 691 were given a prison sentence. Until about October 1961 the SED leadership had largely succeeded in silencing criticism and protest by selective use of the police and the Stasi.

Shots at fugitives

When the borders were shut, numerous East Berliners and GDR citizens began to panic. "It's now or never", many of them said to themselves and made a spontaneous decision to flee. The days and weeks which followed 13th August turned into a macabre contest between fugitives and Border Troops who were trying to make the barbed wire and the wall more and more impenetrable. Those trying to escape, jumped over the barbed wire, crept under fences, broke through the border in vehicles or swam across the Spree and the Teltow Canal. By the middle of September more than 600 people, among them whole families with children, had managed to get to West Berlin using these methods.

There were particularly spectacular escape scenes in Bernauer Straße where the façades of several of the houses formed the sector boundary. Crowds of West Berliners had gathered there and watched as many East Berliners used these buildings to escape. They jumped out of the windows, abseiled off or dropped into the blankets held out by the West Berlin Fire Brigade. Several dramatic situations developed, for example on 24th September 1961, when the police and Stasi tried to pull back a 77 year old woman who had already climbed out of the window. On 22nd August 1961, 59 year old Ida Siekmann jumped out of the third floor of a building on Bernauer Straße and missed the mattress which was being held out and injured herself fatally. On 19th August a 57 year old man suffered terrible wounds from abseiling off and died on 17th September. These fugitives were the first victims of the Berlin Wall.

As a counter-measure, on 24th September the Peoples' Police ordered the 2,000 inhabitants of Bernauer Straße to vacate their homes within four days. The doorways and windows were bricked up. On 15th August journalists in Bernauer Straße were witnesses to a sensational escape. One of the border guards was behaving strangely. He had walked up to the barbed wire barrier several times and pressed it down a bit with his hand. The guard got nearer to the barbed wire, a few minutes passed and then it all happened in a flash. He took a run-up and jumped over the barbed wire, dropped his sub-machine gun whilst he was still in the air and then disappeared in a West

Berlin police van. The picture of the first GDR border guard to escape to the West was flashed around the world.

A total of 18,000 men took part in the building and supervision of the border in August 1961 (NVA, Peoples' Police, members of combat groups, Border Police, Transport Police). They did not know what their task was until they arrived to go into action at the first they had to cope with physical and psychological demands of the job on their own. The heads of operations around Honecker became increasingly worried about the motivation and psychological state of the border guards. There were more and more cases of desertion and moral was not at its highest among the border guards. On 18th August it was reported that the "party political work among the security forces" was still "unsatisfactory"[8]. The reliable propagandist, Karl-Eduard von Schnitzler was posted in immediately to strengthen the shaky ideological attitude of the troops. But even that did not prevent the numbers of deserters from growing.

In the first six weeks after the closing of the border, 85 GDR Border Police fled from East to West Berlin. The high numbers of deserters led to an intensification of the political and ideological training of the Border Troops and a strengthening of controls and sanctions in the Border Regiments. In future, patrols of two to three men were used to ensure mutual checks.

The commands and duty regulations in the months that followed all used clear language. The troops were to shoot "ruthlessly" at "border violators". Following a meeting held on 22nd August 1961 the instruction went out from the SED leadership, "that anyone who violates the laws of our German Democratic Republic will even – if necessary – be brought to order by using weapons."[9] Two days later the first fatal shots were fired.

On the afternoon of 24th August 1961 the 24 year old tailor Günter Litfin ran towards the border under the rail tracks at Friedrichstraße Station. A sentry in the GDR Transport Police (Trapo) ordered him to stop

15th August 1961: Conrad Schumann (2nd from left) is still wrestling with his decision.

and gave two warning shots. Litfin jumped into the water of the Humboldt Port in order to swim across to West Berlin. The statement given by the leader of the Trapo section depicts briefly and coldly what happened next: "After a machine gun salvo of three shots had been fired into the water several metres in front of the border violator and the latter did not turn back, there were two further carefully aimed shots and the border violator went under."[10] Two hours later the body was recovered from the Spree by Vopos. Günter Litfin was the first refugee who was shot and killed at the Berlin Wall.

Escape attempts – termed "border breakthroughs" by the Border Troops – became increasingly more difficult and dangerous. On 29th August a man was shot dead trying to swim down the Teltow Canal. On 13th October a refugee was killed on the Potsdam-Babelsberg border and West Berlin by members of the Transport Police. By the end of October 1961 15 people had met their death on the border with West Berlin.

Each escape attempt was carefully registered by the GDR Border Troops. The means of transport used, for example cars or boats, were recorded as well as the circumstances of the escape. This information was assessed by the military commanders and used as the basis for planning further border fortifications. Although the organisation of the border regime and the strengthening of the border itself progressed rapidly, the troops recorded 216 escape attempts involving 417 people up to 18th September alone. At a meeting of the "Central Staff" on 20th September 1961, Honecker gave a warning in the name of the Politbüro that "the engineering measures to ensure the security of the State Border in Berlin are still inadequate". He instructed the commanders of the Border Troops to take more vigorous action in future. "All breakthroughs must be made impossible."[11] According to the minutes of the Politbüro meeting on 22nd August 1961, all escape attempts should be stopped, even by taking direct aim if there is no alternative method of making an arrest.

The leap into the West – a picture that went around the world. (Photo: Peter Leibing)

"Firearms are to be used against traitors and border violators ... An observation and firing area is to be established in the Border Zone ..."

For the month of October 1961, however, the border troop statistics list a further 85 "border breakthroughs" ("49 minor incidents; 36 serious incidents"), in which 151 people (carefully separated in the files according to sex and age) succeeded in fleeing to West Berlin. Under the heading "direction" there were two columns: "GDR – West" and "West – GDR". The latter, it has to be said, remained empty. The most frequent methods of escape were recorded in the statistics as "cutting" or "crawling under" the wire and "climbing over the Wall". Unquestionably, the duty of the border guards was to prevent "border breakthroughs" and if necessary, to shoot to kill. However, the Party and the military wanted this to be the last resort; any shooting at the

Wall and the inner German border should be avoided wherever possible, not least with a view to the damage that it could cause the international reputation of the GDR. The border security system was therefore constructed to be staggered more deeply and to be more close-meshed so that escapees couldn't even manage to get near the border. In May 1962 a spectacular incident at the Wall turned into a classic shoot-out between GDR border guards and West German policemen. A boy from Thüringen, who was only just 15 years old, Wilfred T., jumped into the Spandau Canal at about 5.45 p.m. in order to swim across to West Berlin. GDR guards opened fire. In spite of several wounds Wilfrid T. was able to reach the other side where a transport worker came to his aid. However, the GDR soldiers kept shooting at the escapee whereupon two West Berlin policemen returned fire. During the heavy gunfire the 21-year old GDR border

Roll call of the "workers' militia" on 23rd August 1961. Ulbricht (front), Honecker (2nd from left) and Verner (4th from left) thank the troops for their "supreme efforts".

guard, Peter Göring, was fatally hit. The
GDR soldiers shot a total of 121 rounds.

In August 1962, a year after the border had
been closed, the agonising death of Peter
Fechter demonstrated the monstrosity of
the Wall to the whole world. Together with
a work-mate the 18-year old apprentice
builder wanted to escape to the West in
Zimmerstraße, very close to Checkpoint
Charlie. They had both already climbed over
the first fence when they were noticed by
the border guards, who shouted at them and
then opened fire. A total of 21 shots were
fired. The friend was able to climb over the
barriers but Peter Fechter had been hit in
the stomach and in the back and lay under
the Wall on the East Berlin side. The GDR
soldiers made no effort to help Fechter, who
was bleeding to death. He was shouting for
help but the West Berlin Police could not get
to him because he was lying on East Berlin
territory. All they were able to do was to

Übersicht über bestätigte Fahnenfluchten

Lfd. Nr.	Datum	Dienstgr.	Name, Vorname	Einheit	flüchtig mit Waffe/Mun.	Wo	Wie
1.	~~12.8. 15.00 h~~	~~Ltn.~~	~~Pilz, Wilfried~~	~~III./Brig.~~ /		/	~~P. verließ am 12.8. - 15 h seine Wohnung~~
2.	15.8. 15.40 h	Owm.	Schumann, Konrad	I.Brig.	mit MPi	Stützpunkt 3 Bernauer - Ecke Rubiner Strasse	Übersteigen der Drahtsperre
3.	16.8. 16.30 h	Uwm.	Oschmann, Helmut	Lehrber.	Leuchtp. 20 Schuss	Schönefelder Str.-Bahnh. Schönefeld	nagelten bei Sperrenbau so, dass immer 100m voraus
4.	16.8. 16.30 h	Uwm.	Phillipeit, Jürgen	Lehrber.	/	dto.	dto.
5.	16.8. 18.00 h	Uwm.	Strauss, Werner	Lehrber.	Karabiner"S" 20 Schuss	Nähe Schönef. Strasse	unter Vorspiegelung Essen zu empfangen und Überprüfung, ob Arbeitsgeräte liegen geblieben, überschritten die Grenze
6.	16.8. 18.00 h	Uwm.	Luding, Klaus	Lehrber.	dto.	dto.	dto.
7.	17.8. 01.20 h	Uwm.	Höhth, Ulli	8. Ber.	mit MPi.	Stützpunkt 10 KP 70 Massantebrücke	Durchkriechen der Drahtsperre
8.	17.8. 01.00 h	Anw.	Dachsel, Günter	9. Ber.	m. Pistole "M"	Stützpunkt 10 Dagmarstieg	Übersteigen des Stacheldrahtzaunes
9.	17.8. 0.30 h	Uwm.	Katzer, Rudolf	I./Brig.	MPi u. 40 Schuss	Koboltwerk, Brunnenstrasse	Übersteigen der Mauer des Betriebes welche gleichzeitig Grenze ist

- 2 -

208

In East Berlin exact accounts were kept of the numbers and circumstances of desertions.

GDR border guards recover the lifeless body of Peter Fechter.

throw him packs of bandages. The American soldiers on duty at Checkpoint Charlie were also afraid to step on to East Berlin territory in order to help the wounded man. Hundreds of people gathered on the West Berlin side of the Wall and shouted in helpless anger and outrage at the GDR guards, demanding them do something to help. They implored the Americans to take some action. But it was all in vain. The two sides faced each other rigidly, waiting to see what would happen: the West Berlin Police who couldn't help and the GDR border guards who didn't want to help or perhaps weren't allowed to help? Between them was the victim whose calls became fainter and fainter. An hour passed and then Peter Fechter's lifeless body was carried away by GDR Border Policemen. No other incident at the Wall enraged the Berliners as much as Peter

25 08 06
264

Ministerium des Innern
Bereitschaftspolizei
  1. Grenzbrigade (B)
- Leiter Operativ -

O.U., den 18.10.1961

HB 30/19 0 15 r 96

An das

Kommando der Bereitschaftspolizei

Leiter Operativ

Oberstleutnant Z i e s c h o w

Betr.: Schußwaffengebräuche bei Grenzdurchbrüchen und versuchten
      Grenzdurchbrüchen in der Zeit vom 13.08. - 10.10.1961

Bezug: Telefonische Anweisung vom 17.10.1961

Z e i t	Warnschüsse	Zielschüsse	erzielte Wirkung
13.08 - 31.08.	3	1	1 Toter
01.09.- 10.09.	-	-	-
11.09.- 20.09.	6	3	2 Verletzte
21.09.- 30.09.	29	10	9 Verletzte
			29 Festnahmen
01.10.- 10.10.	12	4	1 Toter
			2 Verletzte
			11 Festnahmen
Gesamt	50	18	2 Tote
			13 Verletzte
			40 Festnahmen

On 24th August 1961 the first fatal shots were fired at a "Wall fugitive".

Fechter's slow and agonising death. In the days that followed there were angry demonstrations in West Berlin. People were so incensed that they became violent towards Soviet soldiers and threw stones at the bus transporting them to the Soviet Memorial in the Tiergarten. The Allies also bore the brunt of some of the anger; at first they were subjected to verbal abuse and there were even attacks on American military.

Why didn't the GDR border guards help Fechter? One answer to this question is that they were probably too frightened. During the previous weeks two GDR soldiers had been killed by an escapee; one at Check-

point Charlie, exactly the place where Peter Fechter had met his death and another during an exchange of fire with the West Berlin Police. In the summer of 1962 there were feelings of extreme insecurity among the Border Troops.

Peter Fechter's death had led to a change of attitude in the West Berlin population and politicians. The restraint exercised by the Americans had shown that it was primarily the task of the Berlin politicians to take away at least part of the horror of the Wall, by trying to make it less impenetrable. The West Berlin politicians who turned this painful realisation into concrete policies included Willy Brandt, but also Egon Bahr and Heinrich Albertz.

Potsdamer Platz, November 1961. Gradually the Wall also turned into a tourist attraction.

IN THE SHADOW OF THE WALL

Separations

The Wall cut into the flesh of a living city. It separated families, friends and lovers. Before the border was closed, hundreds of thousands of Berliners crossed the sector boundaries every day to visit friends and relatives in another part of the city, to go shopping, to go to the hairdressers or to the cinema. About 12,000 West Berliners worked in the East and 53,000 East Berliners set off every morning to their jobs in the West, often given dirty looks by their neighbours because they were earning "West money" there. The events in August 1961 put an end to all this in one go.

In September 1961 relatives and friends suddenly could have been living on the moon. On 23rd August the last crossing points for West Berliners were closed. The GDR demanded passes from the inhabitants of the West sectors, which they wanted to issue at the Zoo Station, in West Berlin. The West Berlin Senate flatly refused, as this step would have meant that the GDR government would have been able to exercise sovereign rights in the west part of the city.

When the crossing points were closed the last means of contact within the city were cut. There were no telephone connections. Communication with uncles and aunts, grandparents and grandchildren was only possible by exchanging glances or calls over barbed wire and a Wall which kept growing.

It was soon no longer possible to wave or even briefly exchange glances over the Wall. The border installations became more and more impenetrable and the border regime increasingly strict. On 15th August, in many places the GDR began to replace the barbed wire with a Wall. It consisted at first of hollow bricks which were later covered with a layer of concrete slabs. Little by little the sealed border turned into a Wall.

The building of the Wall meant that there was a stabilising process. People could no longer run away. After 13th August, however, the government at first increased repression – in the second half of 1961 18,297 political sentences were passed, in comparison with 4,442 in the first half of the year. Gradually the iron grip was relaxed and when the economic situation and standard of living began to slowly improve from

During the first few weeks the GDR Police still allowed people to wave at each other over the Wall.

1963/64 onwards, many people in the GDR were able to come to terms with their circumstances more easily.

Looking back the author, Günter de Bruyn commented: "In spite of everything, we had to learn to live with the Wall. We couldn't keep calling ourselves indecisive blockheads because we didn't go over to the West in time, we couldn't keep eternally pining for the Kurfürstendamm or the Britz village pond, couldn't continually find it painful to think that we couldn't see the Taunus or the Odenwald ... any longer and that Copenhagen, Paris or Rome were forever denied to us. We had to forget that the bustling Ackerstraße ... continued northwards ..., and whenever we heard the underground trains running under the pave-

The Wall separated this West Berlin bride and bridegroom from the bride's parents.

ments in five minute intervals from West Berlin to West Berlin, at some point we had to stop thinking: Ah, if only we could get on and go to Tegel or Neukölln. In order to live locked up we had to try to live as if the barrier didn't exist."[12]

"Entry" into East Berlin was actually possible without having to show any identity; this was yet another of the many bizarre things about the walled city of Berlin. The S-Bahn station Wollankestraße on the North-South axis was one such example. It was in the East Berlin borough of Pankow, directly on the border with the West Berlin borough of Wedding, and could only be used by West Berliners. There was a sign to warn passengers: "Warning! This entrance and the station are in the Soviet Sector."

"Stop! Border Zone!" – Living and working by the Wall

More than 120,000 people lived and worked on East Berlin and GDR territory in the immediate vicinity of the Wall. 120,000 potential escapees – or perhaps the same number of "Volunteer Helpers of the Border Troops"?

In June 1963 an official "Border Zone" was declared which could only be entered with special permission. It was between 40 metres and 1.5 kilometres wide, calculated from the "Back-up Wall" of the first boundary , which was regarded as the actual Wall by the East Berliners. They never saw the 3.6 metre high concrete Wall which confronted the West Berliners, until 1989.

At some points of the "Outer-ring Border" the Border Zone stretched 2.5 metres

A "volunteer helper" checking a resident's pass in the "Border Zone".

Anyone who lived or worked in the "Border Zone", or who wanted to visit a grave there, had to have a special pass or "grave ticket".

into the surrounding area. There were warning signs saying, "Stop! Border Zone!" Access roads and paths were usually blocked off by "window box barriers". The regulations for access were strictly controlled: "Exceptional access for citizens who have to pass through the protective strip because of their job or to reach their home can only be granted in clearly justified cases."[13]

Spontaneity was never a quality much in demand in the GDR and in the Border Zone it didn't exist at all. Anyone wanting to make a weekend visit to relatives living there, had to register their request with the Peoples' Police and had to wait up to four weeks for permission. There were no special control points but they had to be prepared to show the special pass or "proof of right" at any time to members of the Border Troops, Peoples' Police or the so-called "Volunteer Helpers".

The police passed the requests on to the local Stasi via the Department of the Interior. There, the relevant personal files were carefully checked and the applications had to go back to the police stamped "no problems" or "permission refused" with no explanation provided.

The factories and businesses located in the Border Zone were a particular security problem. The Border Troop Command kept urging for stricter controls: "Security and control measures must be undertaken in factories and other business concerns located

in the Border Zone … so that the property cannot be used for the purpose of violating the border."[14]

Several cemeteries, like the Invaliden and the Sophien cemeteries, were situated in the Border Zone. A special "grave ticket" had to be applied for to enter such cemeteries. Labourers and craftsmen who were working near the Wall had to acquire a green "pass for a temporary stay in the Border Zone."

According to a Defence Ministry list from 1975, for example, a total of 88,579 passes were issued for the Border Zone around West Berlin. When escape attempts by people living in the Border Zone began to increase at the end of 1988, the Border Troop Command demanded that citizens who had applied to leave the country should not be allocated accommodation in the Border Zone and any such applicants already living there should be "relocated".

The GDR leadership wanted the Border Zone to have as few loop-holes as possible and were prepared to use rigorous methods to ensure that this was the case. Buildings were torn down to create a free "observation and firing area" for the Border Troops. In the 1960s in particular, the SED leadership ordered extensive relocation and demolition so that any "blind spots" in the East Berlin inner-city area could be got rid of. Whole blocks of flats and factories were demolished in the wake of these "resolving measures" and the area was subsequently lev-

View from an observation tower. The Border Troops took over 1000 photos to document the route of the Wall.

elled. Several thousand people had to leave their homes.

Living close to the Wall was quite stressful for many people, if not most of those affected. Having the Border Zone right in front of their eyes – lifeless, deserted, dangerous and illuminated at night, and being constantly reminded that what was on the other side was sealed off – who wouldn't find that disturbing? Therefore, alongside the controls and the repression, there were also privileges for those who lived and worked in the Border Zone, including a 15% wage supplement. Areas near the border, particularly the inner German border, but also the Border Zone around West Berlin were always supposed to be "well-supplied". "Safeguarding the supplies of the population living in districts and parishes near the border is a task of primary importance for the trade and service industries. The Borough and District Councils are responsible for gastronomic supplies and care of a high standard."[15]

But the reality often looked quite different. A former inhabitant of the Border Zone: "They may have kept saying that the people in the Border Zone must have preferential treatment because they suffer terrible deprivation, then it was only relative. Many great speeches were made about supplying the Border Zone and the crass comparison was our local department store." In fact, people who lived in the Border Zone had quite a lot to put up with. They were kept under almost total and tiresome surveillance. "Every night the soldiers came and looked in the cellar and in the attic. At 2 a.m. the motorbike with guards stopped outside. They opened up and went down to the cellar. We even had to take up the blanket we'd put in front of the cellar door or make a hole in it so that they could shine a torch in."[16] But despite everything the Border Guards did, they couldn't stop more and more citizens from trying to escape.

Living near the Wall in Teltow. Safe from break-ins – but it must have felt very oppressive at times.

ESCAPE OPERATIONS

Tunnel Escapes

One of them wanted to get his girlfriend out, another had an open dispute with the SED, two joined in for reasons of solidarity and a sense of adventure. Five months after the building of the Wall, Hasso, Ulli, Gigi and Mommo, four students in West Berlin made plans to conquer it. This turned into one of the most spectacular escape attempts of all time and television cameras were there to film it live.

The sewage system could no longer be used because it had now been sealed off with metal gratings. Breaking directly through the border had become more dangerous as several escapees had already been shot. So it had to be a tunnel. For several days the four students searched for suitable terrain on the West Berlin side. Then they found the ideal spot; a half-demolished factory site at 73, Bernauer Straße. First they dug down seven metres deep in the cellar, then straight along. They dug 24 hours a

Framed? Photo from the Border Troop files showing the arrest of a fugitive.

day in three shifts and progressed between one and three metres a day, depending on the soil. 41 men were involved in the operation. An improvised system using a ventilator and oven pipes provided air. Through a journalist the tunnel builders had got in contact with an American television crew who filmed the action from its early stages. They also had to be sworn to secrecy and were driven to Wedding in a VW mini-bus with the blinds drawn down and had to go into the cellar blind-folded. The TV Company NBC paid $12,000 for the exclusive rights to the report – money the tunnel builders badly needed.

At the beginning of September 1962 the breakthrough was made. Now the potential escapees had to be secretly informed and this dangerous task was undertaken by a young woman from West Germany, because citizens of the Federal Republic of Germany were allowed into East Berlin whereas West Berliners weren't. She went into an East Berlin bar and ordered a coffee – the agreed signal. There was no coffee but the fugitives, who had been told to go to the bar, knew this. The young woman downed a brandy and left the bar. The group followed her into the house in Schönholzerstraße.

Hasso was already waiting at the end of the tunnel with a sub-machine gun at the ready. They couldn't be sure who would be standing in front of them when the final barrier fell. Then came the deciding moment. Hasso threw himself against the cellar door. Several people were staring at him anxiously. One after another the fugitives climbed into the tunnel and crawled the 150 metres to the West. Among them were also two small children. On 14th September 1962 a total of 29 people emerged into daylight in Bernauer Straße, covered in dirt but overjoyed. One of the tunnel builders was holding his five-month old son in his arms for the first time and this scene was also captured on film by the NBC television crew.

In the first few weeks after the closure of the border, many people were still taking the direct escape route. The barriers around West Berlin consisted mainly only of barbed wire fences which, in many places, could be breached without too much difficulty, although the consequences might be fatal. They shot to kill but still more people dared to take the risk.

1962/63 was the peak time for the tunnel builders. The first big tunnel success was on 24th January 1962 in Oranienburger Chaussee. After weeks of preparations 28 people crawled under the border into the West. In the spring, not far from this spot, a group of 12 mainly elderly people dug a tunnel 32 metres long and up to 1.75 metres high and, led out by an 81-year old man, arrived in West Berlin on 5th May 1962. In June 1969 a further 25 GDR citizens burrowed their way through to Hermsdorf, Britz and Neukölln in West Berlin.

However, there were soon setbacks. Several projects were discovered in advance by the GDR Border Troops and both the fugitives and their helpers were arrested, usually because their preparations and camouflage procedures had been insufficient. There was also shooting. On 6th October 1962 a West Berliner was gunned down in an exposed tunnel which had been dug from Elsenstraße in Neukölln. A few weeks previously on 18th June 1962, Reinhold Huhn, a GDR Border Guard, was shot dead near Checkpoint Charlie. A 31-year old man, Rudolf M., had dug a 22 metre long tunnel from the Axel Springer building in Kreuzberg, which ended in Zimmerstraße in East Berlin. M. intended to bring his family over to the West through this tunnel. When the group of fugitives approached the tunnel entrance they were stopped by GDR Border Guards. M. fired and the 20-year old soldier, Reinhold Huhn, was fatally wounded.

There were some extremely expert tunnel specialists and one of them was Wolfgang

Fuchs. The press called him "the tunnel fox" and made a great fuss of his achievements in the media. In this early phase the tunnel builders received quite generous financial and material support. The most important sponsors were publishing houses such as the Springer press or the magazine "Stern", which secured exclusive rights for large spreads of photo stories. Using undercover channels, the West Berlin Senate also sometimes provided financial aid. In Autumn 1964 there were already seven tunnel projects which Wolfgang Fuchs was organising together with seven students from the Technical University. They ran a 12 metre long tunnel over to the East from the cellar of a disused bakery in Bernauer Straße. At this stage, like most of the other escape helpers, Fuchs' motives for helping fugitives were mainly idealistic and altruistic. Over months of work, mostly in three shifts around the clock, they dug a tunnel 145 metres long and 70 centimetres high and between 3rd and 5th October, a total of 57 fugitives crawled into the West through the narrow cavity. After three nights the tunnel was discovered by GDR Border Guards and there was an exchange of fire in which the GDR guard, Egon Schultz, was killed.

After these shots at Bernauer Straße the tunnel phase was over. Private sponsors withdrew and political support ceased, not least because of the efforts of both the Senate and the Federal Government to use political means to make the Wall less impenetrable.

In the cellar of this house in Wedding was the end of a tunnel through which 57 fugitives reached the West.

Smuggling and breaking through

From about 1963 onwards, escaping from the GDR required not just courage and imagination but, to an increasing extent, money. About DM 2,000 was paid per fugitive. However, a semi-professional tunnel builder with the code-name "Mr. Big" was not exactly able to get rich on the proceeds. The money went mainly into the building of the particular tunnel for which he charged a total of DM 28,000 to a Stern reporter. And yet helping fugitives gradually became a lucrative business. In West Berlin newspapers obscure small ads appeared, which offered, for example, "Help in family difficulties" with further information available from a box number. In this way contacts were made with West Berliners who wanted to get friends or relatives out of the GDR. The riskier the enterprise, the higher the prices. At the end of the Sixties between DM 15,000 and DM 20,000 per person had to be shelled out.

The professional escape helpers developed more and more sophisticated methods of smuggling people out of the GDR. The most common were specially converted vehicles and foreign passports. The escapees and their helpers were very enterprising when it came to accommodating people in the smallest of hiding places. In 1964, nine people in succession even managed to escape in a BMW Isetta. But escaping in a converted car was particularly dangerous, because GDR Border Guards analysed failed attempts in vehicles in minute detail and then used the information collected to intensify their controls. A report which a Border Brigade prepared for the local SED authorities in Berlin for the year 1966 stated: "Whenever hostile elements have, in some individual cases, succeeded in breaching the State Border we used this opportunity to critically review inadequacies and

problems. This process has opened up new reserves which have been effective in increasing security at the State Border."[17]

It was a dangerous business in which everyone involved was risking a great deal. Despite the most careful preparations and strict conspiracy, many attempts to smuggle people out failed. In addition, the GDR State Security kept managing to smuggle spies into the groups of escape helpers. Captured helpers accused of "criminal trade in human beings" were given long prison sentences. Every arrest and every trial brought new information which the Ministry of State Security evaluated and used to intensify controls. At the end of the Sixties the smuggling started to decrease.

Various kinds of vehicles were used both for smuggling people and for breaking through the border installations. Train driver, Harry Deterling, his stoker and his family succeeded in making a particularly spectacular escape on his steam engine.

In this case, as well, the Border Troops reacted by immediately strengthening their border installations. The railway lines in the vicinity of stations on the border were converted and from 1966 fitted with "protective and derailment points" making it technically impossible for unauthorised trains to go through. In 1966 two East Berliners flattened a section of the Wall with a bulldozer. Although border soldiers immediately opened fire, the men managed to get over to the West with only minor injuries. At the

This advertisement offering to help smuggle people out of the GDR was put up on a viewing platform in Bernauer Straße.

border crossing of Sandkrugbrücke in May 1963, an attempt failed when a bus tried to break through concrete blocks and a barrier and several people were seriously injured. 17-year old Bodo Kunkel in East Berlin also wanted to devise a possible way of leaving the GDR; finally he decided on the largest vehicle that was ever used for an escape – the pleasure steamer "Friedrich Wolf", the flagship of the "Weiße Flotte (White Fleet)" who Kunkel worked for as a seaman. Early in the morning of 7th June 1962 the "Friedrich Wolf" left the Treptow landing stage with Kunkel and a few conspirators in command. The Captain and an engineer lay in the cabin in a drunken stupor having been plied with alcohol and put out of action the night before by the fugitives. Altogether there were twelve of them on board. When they reached Elsenbrücke a police boat pulled alongside. Kunkel showed them the special permit for using the border waters and everything was in order. Shortly afterwards he pulled the rudder sharply to the port side and the "Friedrich Wolf" turned into the Landwehr Canal towards West

Berlin. GDR Border Guards immediately fired at the boat and West Berlin Police gave covering fire. Although the boat was hit, no-one on board was injured. After several nerve-racking minutes Kunkel and his supporting crew reached West Berlin territory.

Another fugitive chose the air as an escape route. Late in the afternoon of 28th July 1965 the Leipzig economist, Heinz Holzapfel locked himself, his wife and his 9-year old son in a lavatory in the East Berlin House of Ministers in Wilhlemstraße. The south wing of the building, formerly the Nazi Air Ministry, today the Federal Finance Ministry, was right next to the Border Zone. After darkness had fallen, Holzapfel hurled a hammer over the Wall which had a thin nylon string attached to it. On the West Berlin side, waiting relatives fastened a steel rope to the thread which Holzapfel carefully pulled towards him. He secured the rope on to a flagpole on the building. The first person to slide down this improvised "cable car" over the Wall was his son, who was tied on with straps. Then followed

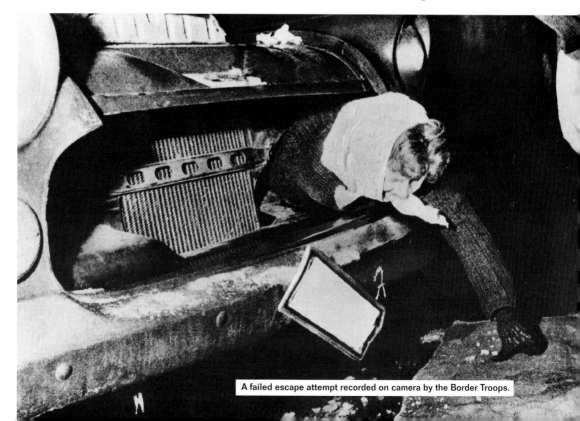

A failed escape attempt recorded on camera by the Border Troops.

his wife Jutta and finally Holzapfel himself. The contraption wasn't discovered by Border Troops until the following morning.

Desertions

Members of the Border Troops often deserted. One of the most spectacular desertions took place in April 1963 when some soldiers broke through the Wall in Berlin-Treptow using a tank and then escaped to West Berlin with several friends on a lorry which followed behind.

At the end of 1963 the National Defence Council decided, among other things, to improve the working conditions of the Border Troops because of the increasing numbers of desertions. Higher wages, improved supplies, better chances of promotion, a comprehensive system of bonuses and increments and the obligation of commanders to treat their subordinates "better" were all included in the measures taken. The number of desertions actually fell, although tighter controls and repressive measures were also brought in alongside the improvements.

The GDR Border Troop desertions in Berlin and at the inner German border totalled 2,800 which included numerous Officers and Commanders.

The whole point of the Wall was to stop people escaping to the West even if SED propaganda constantly referred to the "anti-fascist protective wall" and to the task of repulsing "Western Imperialism".

"Breaking through the border must not be permitted" was the brief but clear central requirement in the basic orders of the Defence Ministry to the border regime. In the West everyone talked about the "Wall and the barbed wire" yet the border soon consisted of many other elements: vehicle barriers, fencing equipped with sensors, service roads, guard dog runs, observation towers, earth bunkers, land and fragmenta-

tion mines – although the latter were only laid on the inner-German border.

Roughly speaking the border installations were reinforced and extended in three stages:

Extension 1 from 1961 to 1968
Extension 2 from 1968/69 to 1980
Extension 3 from 1981 to 1989

On 13th August 1961 the first barriers in Berlin consisted of barbed wire and armed Border Police and workers' militia branches. The building of the Wall started on 15th August. Construction workers erected a Wall out of breeze-blocks and bricks at several places in the inner-city area to about the height of a man. This "first generation Wall", a description used in the West, where a distinction was made between four generations up to 1989, was still irregularly built and on average 30 centimetres thick. Barbed wire at the top was meant to make climbing over difficult. The observation towers were obviously put up quickly and made of wooden beams and panels.

It quickly became clear that the first Wall could not withstand any attempts to break through it with heavy vehicles. Therefore, after a few weeks it was strengthened to a depth of one metre at particularly "dangerous" places by using concrete slabs.

In November 1961 near Checkpoint Charlie, army engineers began to replace the "improvised" first version of the Wall with the "second generation Wall". This was supposed to improve the look of the Wall in places which were particularly exposed to the West, for example at the Brandenburg Gate or at Checkpoint Charlie. This was as an issue which the SED leadership and the Border Command kept returning to over the decades that followed.

At the beginning of 1962 engineering units began to lay a service road along the border reinforcements. Border guards were to become more mobile and if there was a "breakthrough" alert they had to have quick access to the place where it had happened. At the same time the first dog runs were installed.

In the first few months the GDR leaders were still very dissatisfied with the border regime; both with the installations themselves as well as the level of morale and training of the troops. In an order dated 14th December 1961, the GDR Defence Minister Hoffmann spoke his mind: "The organisation of border security does not meet the demands required to prevent border breakthroughs. The combat training required for successful security has been woefully neglected; it is disorganised and of a low standard and has led to deficiencies in the behaviour of soldiers on border duties … . The soldiers must be trained by means of systematic preparation to shoot accurately in all kinds of firing positions, especially at moving targets, by day and night."

Order 101/62 of 23rd November 1962 was even clearer. Here, with reference to the demand for better shooting training, it said that the border guards should be capable of "destroying any stationary or moving target in daylight or at night with the first shot."[18]

In 1963 a Wall of concrete slabs was erected by Border Troop engineers along Ackerstraße.

The 101 Orders were of central significance for the border regime. They were issued by the Minister for National Defence who laid down the regulations for the "engineering works required to reinforce the border installations", as well as for the military and ideological training for the period of one year.

Under the heading "Regulations for the use of weapons for guards, sentries and patrols of the National People's Army (DV – 10/4)", in 1965 the "Handbook for Border Soldiers" published the following requirement: "A weapon may only be used ...
d) at the discretion of guards, sentries and patrols as well as any other person temporarily or permanently carrying arms, if other means are not or are no longer sufficient to prevent actions which are clearly directed towards an act of treason against the Workers and Farmers' State ..."[19]. This meant nothing more than an escape attempt.

In 1991, looking back at the use of firearms, a border officer said: "We had it drilled in daily and it was made quite clear that border violators had to be arrested or destroyed, with the use of our weapons. It was clearly stated in our firing regulations: "Shout out, give a warning shot, then take an aimed shot which prevents the border violator from moving any further."[20]

Taking the deaths of fugitives into account comes from the "Law concerning the State Border of the GDR" of 25th March 1982. Under paragraph 27 ("use of firearms") it says among other things: "... human life is to be spared if possible." If possible.

In reality, however, the guidelines for using firearms lay in a grey zone, in which the lower ranks and, in the last analysis, the border guard himself had the burden of making the actual decision. A former Border Troop Commander stated: "The border guards were given sole responsibility. I imagine this was done on purpose. I never directly ordered them to "shoot at fugitives from the Republic". This was never expressed directly. The buck was passed – right from the top down and stopped with the man who had to stand out there and decide whether to shoot or not."[21]

The end of an escape attempt in the borough of Mitte in 1971.

Reinforcing and improving the border installations

In August 1964, three years after the building of the Wall, the border installations in and around Berlin consisted of the following: the actual Wall had increased in length to 15 kilometres and across a stretch of 130 kilometres were wire fences and barriers. There were a total of 165 observation towers, mainly constructed of wood and 232 bunkers or gun emplacements. The border strip was not yet completely lit and neither was there a complete service road parallel to the border. At this point the costs of the border installations were running at 56.5 million GDR marks.

The Politbüro itself, the highest centre of power of the GDR, dealt with the situation at the Wall and demanded "engineering and military solutions" to deal with the escape operations. In the autumn of 1964 Major General Poppe had to report back to the Politbüro. There was a hail of recriminations because the top GDR brass were extremely disgruntled at the high numbers of escapees and deserters and they were pressing for a further tightening of the border regime. The worried Command Staff of the Border Troops launched into frenetic activity. In February 1965 Poppe submitted detailed planning to the Defence Ministry "about the perspective of the reinforcement and extensions of the border installations" up to 1970. It was a document that indulged in almost too much self-criticism. Following 13th August 1961 the border installations had apparently often been erected, "without the necessary trials and partly with insufficient expertise on the part of the personnel brought in and in places it had very limited effectiveness."

In Berlin there were no land or fragmentation mines or spring-gun installations which kept causing death or serious injury to fugitives at the inner-German border. One of the reasons was that the GDR leadership feared international protest at the use of mines and this would have been particularly strong because of the "narrow" border in Berlin.

Poppe also considered the "political effect" of the border in his report. "The engineering installations often don't contribute to improving the standing of the German Democratic Republic among the

Failed. Two fugitives are led away by GDR border soldiers near the Wall.

general public." Next, the paper on general principles lists the most important methods used by escapees to break through the border barriers:

" – Creeping under, cutting and climbing over the barbed wire: ...

– Climbing over the Wall with help from both sides ... :

– Using vehicles to get near to the State Border."

As a result of these conclusions a total of 161.39 kilometres of installations on the border with West Berlin were to be comprehensively reinforced and improved. The details were as follows:

1. the continuation and refurbishment of the Wall
2. the reinforcement of the border fence
3. traffic humps
4. vehicle chicanes
5. construction of a 121 kilometre long service road
6. border lighting along 151 kilometres
7. erection of 150 new observation towers ("all-round view towers")
8. sentry huts
9. two man bunkers (254)
10. surface barriers
11. 130 kilometres of fencing fitted with sensors
12. 100 kilometres of wire lattice fencing
13. 52.5 kilometres of stretched metal fencing
14. 271 toilets[22]

The total cost of these measures, which were largely carried out, was estimated at 36.98 million GDR marks. That worked out at 224,000 marks per kilometre.

Work soon began. From 1968 the plans started to be translated into far-reaching action. The central measure was the erection of the Third Generation Wall, which consisted of industrially manufactured concrete slabs with joints running horizontally and a pipe along the top. From 1971, as an additional barrier for potential escapees, barbed wire 2.9 metres high ("Border Fence 1") was placed on top. In the seventies the border strip was widened as well and in doing so the rear barrier was moved further and further into the middle of the city to keep fugitives as far as possible from the actual Wall. From 1974 GDR Border Troops erected a so-called "back-up Wall" using border fencing fitted with sensors (Border Fence 74). It was precisely at this point – already between 50 and 70 metres in front of the "Wall" – that the "world ended" for the East Berliners.

What, in the West, was always described as the Wall, or the last "barrier between us and the enemy" as it was called in Border Troop jargon, was never even seen by East Berliners until 1989. When East and West Berliners talked about the Wall they had a picture of completely different things in their minds.

THE WALL BECOMES LESS IMPENETRABLE

Permit Agreements

"The Wall must go" was the constantly repeated maxim of the West Berlin politicians during the first few months of the division of the city. But how could this be achieved in the Cold War situation which in Autumn 1962 had headed for a new climax with the Cuba crisis?

In September 1961 a new note had begun to creep into Willy Brandt's aggressive speeches. Everything had to be done "to ensure that as long as the Wall remains, it is at least not impenetrable". The key words had been spoken; people had to be allowed through.

So the "policy of small steps" started, during which the West had to swallow their pride several times. But they did so to make things better for people. The "other side" as the West called the GDR, also had to make concessions in this arduous process.

The first permit agreement was preceded in December 1963 by extremely delicate negotiations and a very complicated system of issuing permits was set up. GDR postal workers accepted the applications in West Berlin, they were processed in East Berlin and then issued in 12 West Berlin schools and sports halls. Long queues formed in front of the West Berlin issuing points and people withstood the snow and the cold for hours in order to acquire the sought-after permits.

Hardly anyone had dared hope, but it had happened at last. For the first time in two years West Berliners were allowed over to their friends and relatives in the East Ber-

The visitors' permit agreement at Christmas 1963: tearful reunions at Friedrichstraße Station.

lin. There were tearful reunions. At the crossing points heavily-laden West Berliners fell weeping into the arms of their relatives. On special request West Berliners could even use their cars, which were an unusual sight on the streets of East Berlin.

At two of the five border-crossing points, Friedrichstraße Station and Oberbaum-brücke, the GDR authorities had built whole forests of processing huts to cope with the expected onslaught. The correct, even polite, manners of the GDR control officials were noticeable. American journalists described it as an almost "Warm Welcome to West Berliners campaign": "The border guards demonstrated how quickly and smoothly pedestrians and vehicles could be processed." Other reports stated: "The border guards involved staged a politeness contest".

The possible dates for visiting East Berlin were severely restricted, from 19th December 1963 to 5th January 1964. In these two weeks a total of 1,242,800 permits for a one-day stay were issued. The permit was valid from 6 a.m. to midnight and DM10 had to be exchanged at a rate of 1:1.

The West "policy of small steps" which required a lot of staying power and the amount of tolerance necessary to withstand many frustrations, had borne its first fruits. At least the Wall had become somewhat less impenetrable, if only in one direction.

In East Berlin the Ministry of State Security had taken overall control of the practical aspects of the second permit agreement at Christmas 1964. "Operation Guest", as it was called, was precisely planned by the Stasi, the Ministry of the Interior and the Ministry for Post and Telecommunications who co-ordinated the whole process between them, from the distribution of the application forms to the statistical evaluation of the permits. In the run-up numerous "IM's" (unofficial collaborators) were to ascertain the "atmosphere among the opera-

tional troops" and "the effects ... of attempts at subversion from the West."

There were four permit agreements in total, the last at Easter 1966. Further visiting regulations broke down because of demands by East Berlin, to which the Senate could not agree for reasons of status rights. The eastern part of the city was once again sealed off to West Berliners. However, from 1964 a "Permit Office for urgent family occasions" was in operation which issued visitor permits for the births, weddings, serious illnesses and deaths of close relatives.

"Border Crossers"

Another political aspect of the Wall was that it created distinctions. Right from the start the border had remained passable for certain groups of people although citizens of East Berlin and the GDR as well as those from East Bloc countries, and for many years West Berliners as well, were not allowed through. Foreigners and West Germans could go through the crossing points to East Berlin, as well as members of the Allied Forces and their families. The Wall was not a barrier to accredited Diplomats in East Berlin either. Some of them used this opportunity to earn themselves extra income by undertaking small or large smuggling activities . Up to the 1970s an estimated total of 2,000 people got across to West Berlin in the boot of a diplomatic car, more or less right under the eyes of the State Security passport control units. Of course, they had some idea of the smuggling that was going, on but weren't allowed to undertake any checks because of the diplomatic status of the border crossers. From the mid-seventies the Wall stopped being an impassable barrier for some GDR actors, musicians and writers. Among the privileged were the writers, Jurek Becker, Rolf Schneider and Heiner Müller, not least because of the income in foreign currency that they could earn in the West as artists who were an embarrassment in their own country.

Someone who crossed the border every day was Friedrich Kittlaus, top S-Bahn man since1949. Kittlaus kept his post even after August 1961, although the SED viewed him as politically rather unreliable. His expertise made him indispensable, so even after the building of the Wall, Kittlaus was allowed to travel daily from his home in West Berlin by chauffeur driven car to his office in East Berlin, without any checks and he remained head of the S-Bahn until his retirement.

Not only Kittlaus, but a whole string of East Berlin S-Bahn employees regularly crossed the border to mend the tracks in West Berlin or to maintain the signal instal-lations. Obviously, careful checks had been made on the people who were allowed to work in West Berlin: no relatives in the West, snow-white personal files, fathers of families preferred. A ten-page questionnaire

was supposed to supply information about, "a strongly-held class position and loyalty to Party and Government". Those selected were given an identity card concerning their "special duty task" and had to report back again at a given time at Friedrichstraße Sta-tion, otherwise an "internal investigation" would be initiated.

Ghost Stations

The twisted geography of the divided city meant that the West Berlin S-Bahn and two of the underground lines ran under East Berlin. Immediately after the closure of the border, the stations lying on East Berlin ter-ritory were shut; all entrances were barred with iron railings and later they were bricked up. The S-Bahn signs and stairwells stood as witnesses to a distant past in the East Berlin streets. For East Berliners the Wall began here at the sealed off S-Bahn entrances, but the trains still ran between the West Berlin boroughs. Most (West) pas-sengers were overcome by uneasy feelings

Laden with gifts, visitors from West Berlin stream towards their relatives.

when they saw the deserted platforms of Nordbahnhof, Oranienburgerstraße, Unter den Linden and Potsdamer Platz disappearing in the dirty yellow light. In the S-Bahn trains conversations became subdued when they drove through the dimly-lit "ghost stations" at a reduced speed. Where there was once the hectic bustle of life in a world city, there were now only extinct platforms, rotting benches and façades. Here the Wall had forced time to stand still.

In some places the signs and advertisements from summer 1961 could still be seen: "RIWA Toilettte-Seifen", "Großhandelskontor Technik", "Richtung Stalinallee-Lichtenberg", "Richtung Bernau". But the connections did not exist any more. You could just see the shadowy figures of border soldiers with their guns slung over their shoulders, scrutinising the trains as they rolled past.

There were 15 of these "ghost stations" on the East Berlin underground. Border Troops and Transport Police made sure that they were completely sealed off, although there were a few special "security problems". A high-ranking Border Troop Officer later described "border security" at these stations as follows: "Our guards were actually walled-in on some stations, like at Potsdamer Platz. They stood on the station inside walls with observation slits. This was partly so that they wouldn't desert and partly so that they weren't subjected to any provocation if an S-Bahn train stopped and some drunks got off … No guard could leave his post unnoticed. But that was in the eighties when things had been tightened up. A the beginning the guards walked up and down the platform because they weren't in the bunkers."[23]

Ex-Major Helmut H. gave this report about guard duty at Potsdamer Platz Station. "You could get lost on Potsdamer Platz Station. And sometimes things were thrown out of the trains. Bottles and all sorts of things. We stood behind pillars or sat in rooms with the doors shut and had to pick

Behind walls with observation slits on the "ghost station" at Potsdamer Platz.

up everything lying around on the ground. The soldiers watched people travelling past in another world. When you had to squeeze yourself into a corner when the train went past, it was a strange feeling."[24]

Friedrichstraße Station

The Wall created paces with a heavily oppressive atmosphere and a haunting inscrutability. They exuded a feeling of indeterminate threat and of being at the mercy of the control and despotism of a suspicious and hostile State. One such place was Friedrichstraße Station, a former junction for S-Bahn, underground and international trains. Here the "Wall" ran between two platforms. A metal partition divided the area with the S-Bahn trains travelling to the West (platform B) and the international platform A from the "East" platform.

For East Berliners S-Bahn platform C meant: "Train terminates here. All passengers alight here, train is going back to Erkner." In 1982 the three metre high wired glass partition was replaced by a steel wall which reached up to the station roof. A white line stretched along the international platforms: "Do not step across this line until instructed". Here, literally every step was observed by the border guards.

Visitors from the West regularly became disorientated in the maze of corridors, steps, passport and customs channels and hidden passageways. It was even difficult for the "border officials of the GDR" to keep track of things in this labyrinth. Visitors entering and leaving the station had to complete an obstacle race, constantly watched by the omnipresent guards and also video-cameras, which were introduced at the beginning of the 80s. As soon as visitors entered the "clearance area" they were sorted into "citizens of West Berlin", "citizens of the Federal Republic of Germany" and "citizens of other States". Now and then there were

envious looks as someone quickly disappeared into the bay for "Diplomats".

Passport and identity card control was the responsibility of the Ministry of State Security. At the border crossings (Grenzübergansstellen = "GÜST") it was the Stasi who actually called the shots. The "passport control units" were directly answerable to the Stasi so that all traffic going both ways at the Wall and at the inner-German border was overseen by Stasi officials.

Friedrichstraße Station was a permanent building site. Alterations were constantly in progress, a door being bricked up or a new entrance being built in order to perfect control over people coming in and out. And then there was something at Friedrichstraße Station that became a firm favourite with many West Berliners: the "Intershop". This was conveniently situated on the S-Bahn platform for the West Berlin lines so that whilst changing trains, passengers could buy cigarettes and spirits at fantastically low duty-free prices, without going through

Patrol on Potsdamer Platz S-Bahn Station. The trains travelled from West to West without stopping.

any immigration formalities and almost without risk, as the West Berlin customs were not allowed to make any checks before the West Berlin stations. A regular "spirits and cigarettes tourism trade" soon developed which blessed the S-Bahn line between Lehrter Station(West) and Friedrichstraße with an unusually large number of passengers. It was a booming business for the GDR, getting rid of tons of cheaply imported West products in exchange for West marks.

From 1962 people leaving East Berlin had to queue up in a newly erected building in front of the station ("Clearance building for departures") where queues frequently stretched out on to the station square. The nickname "Palace of Tears" was only too fitting for this prime example of GDR architecture which looked unusually spacious from the outside but was sterile and oppressive inside.

A new policy for the East: The Four Powers Agreement

When Willy Brandt stepped up to the lectern of the Bundestag as the first Social Democrat Federal Chancellor in October 1969 and gave his inaugural speech, there was a palpable sense of an historic moment. "Let us risk more democracy" was the slogan within the Socialist-Liberal govern-

ment and in the world outside, this turned into "reconciliation with the East". A new "Ostpolitik" (Policy for the East) was the order of the day. Things had brightened up on the international political front. In October 1964 Nikita Khrushchev had been toppled by Leonid Brezhnev, which certainly didn't mean liberalisation for the Soviet Union, but Brezhnev didn't want any trouble abroad. The signs all seemed to point to détente. US President Richard Nixon travelled to Peking and Moscow and in 1969 both Superpowers went into negotiations on arms controls. Even in Berlin a certain normality was to return. The adversaries in the Cold War seemed to be tired of quarrelling about the divided city and had settled for the status quo.

In March 1970 negotiations began between the ambassadors of the USA, Great Britain, France and the Soviet Union in the former Allied Control Building in Berlin-Schöneberg. The constant disputes about questions of status and controls of rights of access were to be put aside. There was hard bargaining behind locked doors, but also a clear desire for agreement. That in itself distinguished the discussions from many of the fruitless Berlin negotiations of the past. On 3rd September 1971 the Four Powers Agreement was signed.

The Four Powers Agreement and the Transit Agreement subsequently negotiated between Bonn and the GDR made life a great deal easier for the West Berliners. After six years, visits to East Berlin were possible again. Following the Four Powers Agreement East Berlin and the West Berlin Senate negotiated a ruling on visitor permits so that they were no longer for specific days. From 1988 on West Berliners were allowed to visit East Berlin for a total of 30 days per year at a pre-arranged crossing point. However, they had to leave before midnight. On 1st July 1982 the final curfew became 2 a.m.

Passport and customs control in the labyrinth of Friedrichstraße Station.

In 1984 the number of possible visits per West Berliner was raised to 45 a year. From 1988 two day visits, which included an overnight stay, were allowed in East Berlin and entry was possible through any chosen crossing point (except Checkpoint Charlie) on foot, by S-Bahn, underground or by car. Soon the GDR discovered a means of controlling the flow of visitors to East Berlin: the level of the "minimum exchange", which was called "compulsory exchange" in the West. As the numbers of visitors grew too alarming they raised the amount of money which had to be exchanged. In 1972 each border crossing cost DM 5 per person at a rate of 1:1. In 1980 the amount was raised to DM 25 which led to a drastic reduction in the number of visitors – from 3.03 million in 1979 to 1.5 million in 1981. After the "agreement on facilitating and improving the flow of visits" in June 1972, the West Berliners made between 3.3 million (1976) and 1.5 million (1983) visits to East Berlin.

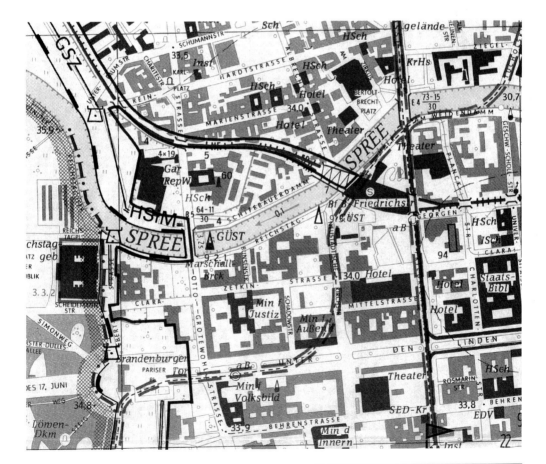

Border Troop map of the Brandenburg Gate area.
GSZ: Border security fence. HSiM: Back-up Wall.

STRENGTHENING THE WALL

"Low maintenance and elegantly proportioned" – Border Wall 75

The Four Powers Agreement of 1971 and the Basic Treaty in 1972 improved the everyday situation of the Berliners and in the final agreement in Helsinki obliged the Eastern Block States to uphold citizens' and human rights. But whilst the policy of détente between East and West made slow progress, the GDR reinforced their borders.

In May 1974 the Border Troop leadership gave instructions for the development of a new kind of Wall. Breaking through the Wall, particularly by means of vehicles, was to be made more difficult and the appearance of the Wall was also given consideration. "The outward appearance of the Wall in the section of the Capital of the GDR must correspond to the standards of the extension of the State border".

Extending and perfecting the border installations was supposed to make them as secure as possible, but at the same time the repulsive military character of the border was to be gradually replaced by a "sterile" border where there were as few incidents as possible. In the Border Troops' files the order crops up time and again to shape the border regime in such a way the "opponent" has as little cause as possible for "stirring up hatred" against the GDR.

The new Wall consisted of 3.6 metre (type UL 12.41 or 12.11) or 2.4 metre high (type UL 8.21) smooth concrete segments 15 centimetres wide which a heavy lorry would be unable to break through. The protruding "foot" was sunk 2.1 metres into the ground and guaranteed a high degree of stability. Crawling under the Wall was practically impossible and climbing over it with ladders or other equipment was also made more difficult because of its increased

In 1966 the "3rd Generation" Wall was erected at Potsdamer Platz using individual concrete segments.

height and the asbestos and concrete piping placed on top. A coat of plain white paint was also planned; the border was to be hygienically clean, to "correspond with the standards required for the section of Wall in the Capital of the GDR".

In 1976 the gradual erection of Border Wall 75 started on the inner-city boundary and from then on it shaped the image of the Wall all over the world. Up to the year 1989 a total of 45,000 concrete segments at an official price of 359 GDR marks, were used to surround West Berlin. At the same time, the elements of the border which had a particularly aggressive effect, for example the concrete humps or "surface barriers" (metal gratings with spikes, laid on the ground) were removed in order to, "continue to raise the political image of Berlin, the Capital of the GDR, at the Brandenburg Gate and the Leipzigerstraße sections which have public appeal"[25].

"Order and cleanliness" were frequently an issue for Border Troops. Commander Baumgarten managed to describe the "Border Wall 75" in an official report as

"low maintenance and elegantly proportioned."[26] The extension and reinforcement of the border installations always took place in overlapping phases. Older elements weren't just replaced in one go by completely new ones. In places, old elements remained standing for years after the "successor type" had to a large extent been installed. The Berlin Wall was never standardised at any one time. In 1990 when the border was being dismantled, here and there demolition troops found concrete posts originating from the year 1961.

In 1983 the inner-city border consisted of the following elements:
– Border Wall 75 (20.1 kms)
– Border fence 83 (10.4 kms)
– Border fencing fitted with sensors (33.3 kms)
– Vehicle barriers (21.5 kms)
– 18,800 surface barriers (metal gratings with spikes, laid on the ground)
– Back-up Wall (27.2 kms)
– Back-up fence (2.8 kms)
Guarding the border included permanent patrols, mostly consisting of two border

Aerial view of the border strip between Mitte and Kreuzberg, with St. Thomas's Church in the foreground.

soldiers, which took place at irregular intervals both on the "death strip" and in front of the back-up Wall. Fugitives weren't supposed to be able to work out the rhythm of the patrols.

In this improvement stage, which started in the mid-seventies, the "order to shoot" was expressly reinforced. At a meeting of the National Defence Council in 1974 the new SED leader, Honecker, who had taken over from Ulbricht in May 1971, gave the clear instruction. "If there are attempts to break through the border, weapons must continue to be used ruthlessly and comrades who have used them successfully are to commended."[27] The commendations consisted of several days special leave, medals and a bonus of between 150 and 500 marks.

The Border Troops of the GDR

On 15th September 1961, four weeks after the Wall went up, the National Defence Council gave instructions for the "Border Troops of the GDR" to be formed from the "German Border Police". They were part of the forces of the National People's Army and were under the command of the Defence Ministry with its Headquarters in Strausberg. The 40,000 strong Border Police had been under the command of the Ministry of the Interior.

In the middle of the 60s the Border Troops of the GDR consisted of ten Border Brigades, each with between two and five regiments. At first, three Brigades were stationed on the border with West Berlin, six on the inner-German border and on the Baltic coast was the "6th Border Brigade – Coast". Until the beginning of the 70s the Border Troops were supplied with tanks of type T34/85, flack, anti-tank cannons and grenade throwers, as well as carbines, submachine guns light MG's, pistols and hand grenades.

These weapons were completely in keeping with the "battle task" spread by propaganda, which was to a stop a possible attack on the border by the "imperialist opponent" from the West. They also justified the significance of the Wall as an "anti-fascist protective Wall" to their own troops and the combat training, including manoeuvre scenarios, was also partly geared to them. The Border Troops in and around Berlin were even trained to fight in houses and on the street. There were actually detailed plans in the safes belonging to the Border Troop Command for a possible military occupation of West. Setting up collective camps for "detaining enemy forces" had even been thought of and there was a special order to be awarded for "heroic deeds" performed in the capturing of Berlin.

After the introduction of National Service in the GDR in January 1962, an increasing number of National Servicemen were drafted into the Border Troops. Great care was taken to ensure that these recruits didn't have relatives in the West or other West contacts. In the first years after the building of the Wall the GDR leadership continued to feel unhappy, even seriously worried, about morale within the Border Troops. Both the "political attitude" of many border soldiers, as well as the discipline, left much to be desired in the opinion of the SED top brass. In addition, up to 1964 the number of deserters steadily rose. To the middle of 1963 alone, 750 desertions were recorded, including 50 at the Berlin Wall.

In response to this situation a whole raft of measures was introduced at the end of 1962. They included privileges, such as better chances of promotion, higher wages, a system of bonuses and additional pay as well as more intensive ideological training and increased repression. The Ministry of State Security placed "unofficial collaborators" in all Border Troop units to monitor their politics and ideology and to expose any escape planes. These Stasi collaborators, who formed the "Administration 2000" had a say in personnel matters as well, for example in the composition of patrols. This surveillance system was constantly extended so that, on average, by the 80s one border soldier in ten was a Stasi informer. One of their tasks was smuggle GDR spies through the border into West Germany.

From January 1974 the Border Troops were no longer officially part of the NVA, but were under the command of the Ministry for National Defence. By formally detaching them, the GDR wanted to make sure that the Border Troops were not an issue in the negotiations on arms limitations in Vienna in 1973.

It wasn't an easy task, motivating the Border Troops for duty at the Wall. Although it was described as an "anti-fascist protective Wall" against the "enemy" in the West, anyone could see that the border installations were, in truth, there to prevent people escaping from the East. Both soldiers and officers had to cope with this contradiction and had to be prepared to and capable of shooting at fugitives if the situation arose. That is why the political and ideological training of the troops came to have such central significance within the border regime.

Specially trained propagandists were sent to the Border Regiments for "ideological reinforcement" and right from the start, Karl-Eduard von Schnitzler tried to underline the necessity of the Wall with particular zeal.

A solid political and ideological world view and a clear picture of the enemy on the basis of Marxism-Leninism were the main elements of "arming the Border Troops from within". The main enemy was "International Imperialism" i.e. the Western States. "As long as Imperialism exists, irreconcilable enmity against Socialism will be the leitmotiv of its politics. It will continually try to penetrate our solid border regime in order to break through our State border, to carry out provocation attacks and, when the moment seems right, to provoke aggression."

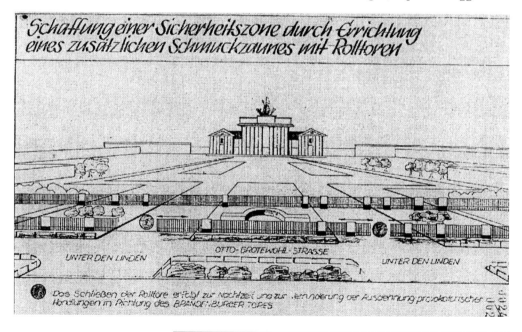

"Order and cleanliness": A GDR sketch of the new lay-out of Pariser Platz, 1983.

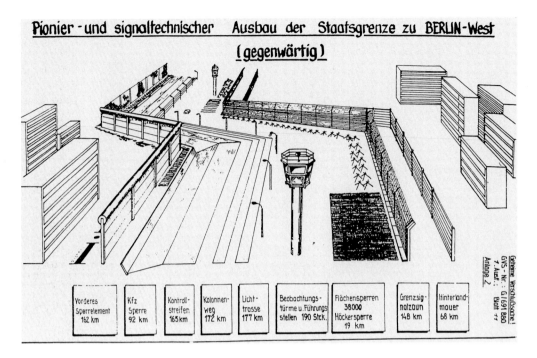

Pionier - und signaltechnischer Ausbau der Staatsgrenze zu BERLIN-West (gegenwärtig)

Vorderes Sperrelement 162 km	Kfz Sperre 92 km	Kontroll- streifen 165 km	Kolonnen- weg 172 km	Licht- trasse 177 km	Beobachtungs- türme u. Führungs stellen 190 Stck.	Flächensperren 38000 Höckersperre 19 km	Grenzsig- nalzaun 148 km	Hinterland- mauer 68 km

Geheime Verschlußsache!
GVS - Nr.: G1 691 880
7. Ausf.:
Anlage 2   Blatt 11

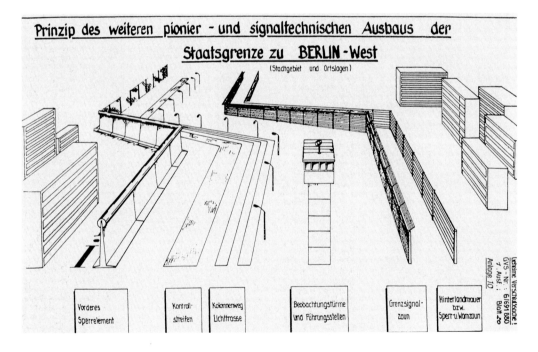

Prinzip des weiteren pionier - und signaltechnischen Ausbaus der Staatsgrenze zu BERLIN - West
(Stadtgebiet und Ortslagen)

Vorderes Sperrelement		Kontroll- streifen	Kolonnenweg Lichttrasse	Beobachtungstürme und Führungsstellen	Grenzsignal- zaun	Hinterlandmauer bzw. Sperr-u.Warnzaun

Geheime Verschlußsache!
GVS - Nr.: G1 691 880
7. Ausf.:
Anlage 10   Blatt 20

Border Troop plans for the border installations in the mid-seventies (above) and plans for further improvements (below). Some elements were removed and the lay-out was clearer.

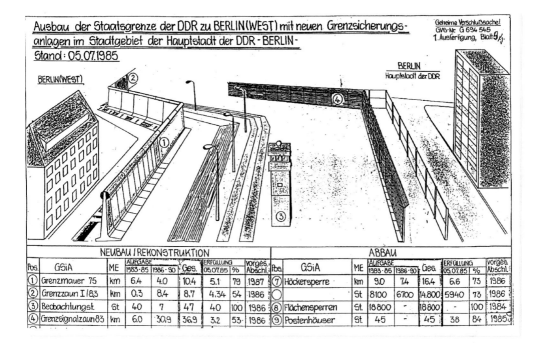

Ausbau der Staatsgrenze der DDR zu BERLIN(WEST) mit neuen Grenzsicherungsanlagen im Stadtgebiet der Hauptstadt der DDR - BERLIN-
Stand: 05.07.1985

Geheime Verschlußsache!
GVS-Nr: G 684 545
1.Ausfertigung, Blatt 9/

BERLIN(WEST)

BERLIN
Hauptstadt der DDR

		NEUBAU / REKONSTRUKTION								ABBAU						
Pos.	GSiA	ME	AUFGABE 1983-85	1986-90	Ges.	ERFÜLLUNG 05.07.85	%	vorges. Abschl.	Pos.	GSiA	ME	AUFGABE 1983-85	1986-90	Ges.	ERFÜLLUNG 05.07.85	%	vorges. Abschl.
①	Grenzmauer 75	km	6.4	4.0	10.4	5.1	79	1987	⑦	Höckersperre	km	9.0	7.4	16.4	6.6	73	1986
②	Grenzzaun I/83	km	0.3	8.4	8.7	4.34	54	1986	○		St	8100	6700	14.800	5940	73	1986
③	Beobachtungst.	St	40	7	47	40	100	1986	⑧	Flächensperren	St	18800	-	18800	-	100	1984
④	Grenzsignalzaun83	km	6.0	30.9	36.9	3.2	53	1986	⑨	Postenhäuser	St	45	-	45	38	84	1985

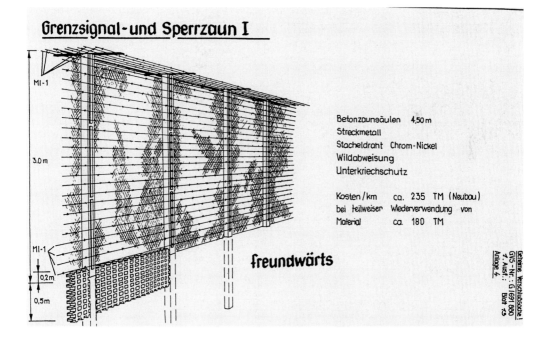

Grenzsignal- und Sperrzaun I

MI-1

3.0 m

MI-1

0,2m

0,5m

Betonzaunsäulen   4,50 m
Streckmetall
Stacheldraht   Chrom-Nickel
Wildabweisung
Unterkriechschutz

Kosten / km   ca. 235 TM (Neubau)
bei teilweiser   Wiederverwendung von
Material   ca. 180 TM

freundwärts

Geheime Verschlußsache!
GVS - Nr.: G 1691 880
7. Ausf.:
Anlage 4
Blatt 15

Border Troop plans of the changes made from 1985 onwards.

Sketch of the barbed wire fence fitted with alarms, which formed the second barrier behind the "Back-up Wall".

This assessment in the 1971 "Guide to Argumentation" for Politics Officers formally covers all the political material required for the political training of the Border Troops. The Training Guidelines for 1975 go on to say: "The reactionary nature and aggressive policies of Imperialism must be exposed more effectively and a class-conscious picture of the enemy must be given to all members of the Border Troops."

A clear image of the enemy was also drawn from within in relation to "opponents of the system" and "fugitives from the Republic". In official Border Troop reports, fugitives were often declared to be "criminals", "traitors" or "opponents" in order to lower the level of inhibition felt by border guards about using their guns. An escape attempt, the confrontation between border guard and fugitive, was frequently described as a "war", as if the guard and fugitive were in a battle situation, where the use of weapons seemed natural.

In 1971, the Central Command sent this message of greeting to the VIIIth SED Party Congress: "Through our very high achievements we have proved our faith in the clear aims of SED policy ... our hatred of Imperialism and its mercenaries..."[28]

Hatred was a leitmotiv of the political training, hatred of both Western Imperialism, the "class enemy", as well as of mercenaries which ultimately included "fugitives from the Republic" and "border violators". In a speech made at the 35th Anniversary of the Border Troops in November 1981, their Commander, Baumgarten, spoke of "contempt and hatred .... against all unprincipled elements ... who are jeopardising the future of the whole of mankind for imperialist interests of profit and power."

Dead Heroes: The cult of the killed border soldiers

Between 1961 and 1989 27 border soldiers were killed at the Wall and the inner-German border whilst using their weapons during escape operations. In the same period 800 fugitives lost their lives. Two of the victims in the Border Troops were particularly distinguished in GDR propaganda: Peter Göring and Reinhold Huhn, both shot dead at the Berlin Wall in 1962. Peter Göring was fatally hit by a bullet from the West on 23rd May 1962 near the Invaliden cemetery in an exchange of fire between GDR guards and West Berlin Police, who were giving covering fire to a 14-year old fugitive.

Reinhold Huhn died on 18th June 1962 near Checkpoint Charlie. Huhn was check-

Border Troop archive photo: Motor cycle patrol on night duty.

ing up on several people who were about to flee through a tunnel into the West, when one of the escape helpers drew his weapon and killed the border guard. Reinhold Huhn and Peter Göring were made "socialist heroes". A memorial was erected to them and other border guards who were killed in the East Berlin borough of Mitte within sight of the Axel Springer building in West Berlin. Border recruits, foreign delegations, children and young people were all taken to see this memorial in Schützenstraße, which was renamed Reinhold Straße. In 1972 the Commander of the Border Troops ordered a "Memorial Room" to be set up in the barracks of the killed border soldiers, in which their portraits and personal belongings were exhibited. Strict orders were given as to the lay-out of these rooms which had to follow a given pattern illustrated by photos and sketches on papers attached to them. In this way the "brutality and ruthlessness" of fugitives from the Republic and of "ene-

mies" on the other side of the Wall were supposed to be demonstrated to the soldiers. Legal investigations after the fall of the Wall indicated that nine border soldiers were probably shot by escaping comrades and in three cases the fatal shots came from the weapons of US soldiers or West Berlin policemen. Whatever the precise circumstances of these deaths, in political-ideological propaganda, they were central to a hero cult which was meant to make border guards conscious of the danger of the job and the treacherousness of the "enemy" – whether fugitives or West Berlin policemen.

Volunteer Helpers of the Border Troops

It was the dream of the GDR leadership – a whole population devoted to protecting the border. It was revealed in 1989 that the Stasi had come a long way with their spying; they had 150,00 unofficial collaborators

Whenever the troops needed an ideological boost, Karl-Eduard von Schnitzler (standing) was always called in.

throughout the GDR. They fell back on the active co-operation of these civilians to keep the border regime intact and prevent escape attempts. These "Voluntary Helpers of the Border Troops", mainly undertook patrol duties in areas near the border where they were supposed to track down potential escapees before they got to the border and hand them over to the People's Police.

It is clear from the statistics provided by the Border Troops that the Volunteer Helpers did a good job acting in combination with the police and the troops. For example, at the inner-German border, including the Berlin Wall, between December 1974 and November 1979 4,956 "movements of persons in the direction GDR–FRG", i.e. escape attempts, were recorded. 3,984 people were arrested before they reached the first fence fitted with sensors and the Volunteer Helpers were largely responsible for these arrests. In the area of the actual border installations in the same period there were a total of 743 arrests by Border Troops. 229 people succeeded in fleeing to the West.[29]

A report by the Border Brigade entitled "13th August" (area of Potsdamer Platz/ Brandenburg Gate) to the Berlin Headquarters of the SED for the period 1965/66, expressly emphasised the part played by people living near the border and by Volunteer Helpers in border security. "With the support of the border population seven people were arrested who were in the Border Zone preparing criminal acts. The help of volunteers has become an important element in the border security system."[30] A former Border Troop Officer described their duties in the following way: "They ... usually did their rounds in the day during working hours or in the evening ... They had to do a patrol, check order and security in the Border Zone ... We felt that the border could only be secure if the population helped us."[31]

The role of the Volunteer Helpers was repeatedly stressed in the 101 Orders, issued by the Defence Minister which annually laid down the guidelines for reinforcing the border regime. "Through the good co-operation of Border Troops ... with the border popula-

View from an observation tower on the border strip at Potsdamer Platz, with the Reichstag in the background.

tion their permanent support of border security can be guaranteed. We must pay great heed to the work of Volunteer Border Helpers (training deployment and allocation of responsibilities)."[32]

In the official "Handbook for Border Soldiers" the tasks and skills of border Volunteer Helpers were described as follows: "The Volunteer Helpers could make a contribution in fulfilling certain primary tasks. They could:

– seek out suspicious persons as well as ... provisionally arrest border violators
– control the traffic at important access points to the Border Zones as well as observe particular locations
– safeguard important factories and property
– reinforce border security and help in the search for border violators who have broken through security.[33]

In August 1952 three months after the inner-German border had been sealed, Border Police at the time had already enlisted 540 civilian "Border Police helpers" for patrolling and observation duties along the demarcation line. From 1958 onwards "Volunteer Helpers of the Border Troops" were recruited who wore civilian clothes and could be distinguished by an armband. The duty of the "helpers", who were attached to one of the Border Regiments, consisted above all in patrolling the area in front of the border installations. They mainly moved about in pairs, or occasionally in groups of up to six people, sometimes accompanied by a member of the Border Police. They were unarmed and either wore civilian clothes with an armband ("Volunteer Helper of the Border Troops") or a uniform consisting of dungarees and a cap. They were supposed to do six to eight hours of duties per month, with special instructions to "reconnoitre and check possible hiding places, building sites, property, factory plants." They had authority to check and detain suspicious persons. The majority of the Volunteer Helpers were recruited from the personnel of factories and businesses near the border in Berlin and the surrounding area. They were all SED Party members and mostly reservists of the Army or the Border Troops.

"Young Pioneers" at the Reinhold Huhn Memorial.

Their induction programme included political and ideological instruction as well as firing and close combat training and lessons in first aid. Their "effectiveness" can be indirectly assessed from the statistics on arrests made in the Border Zone. In 1988 there were a total of 2978 arrest of fugitives on the inner-German border and the Wall:

978 by the People's Police
526 by the Transport Police
614 by Border Troops
273 by the Stasi.[34]

The high number of arrests by the People's and Transport Police was partly due to the information and activities of the Volunteer Helpers.

In 1986 the National Defence Council established an order of the "Volunteers" which was awarded for "loyal services in the protection of the GDR State border." It included a bonus of 150–500 marks. Prizes and bonuses were also awarded for "individual achievements", especially for the arrest of a fugitive.

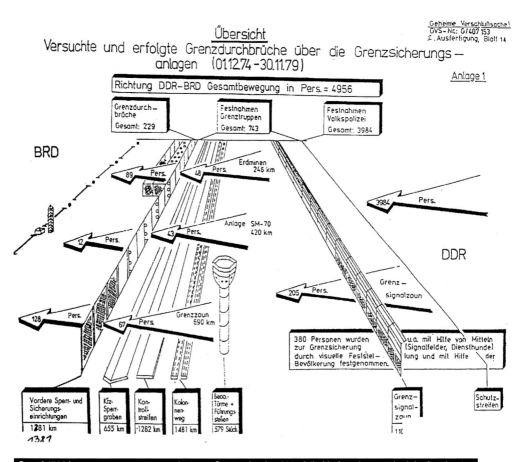

Übersicht
Versuchte und erfolgte Grenzdurchbrüche über die Grenzsicherungs –
anlagen (01.12.74 – 30.11.79)

Geheime Verschlußsache!
GVS-Nr: G/407 153
2. Ausfertigung, Blatt 14

Anlage 1

Richtung DDR–BRD Gesamtbewegung in Pers. = 4956

Out of 4596 known escape attempts at the inner German border, 3984 failed before they reached the first barrier.

A HUNDRED YEAR WALL?

The Wall as a fact of everyday life

Did people gradually get used to the Wall? From the middle of the seventies this was the impression you got in West Berlin, at least. The Wall and the division of the city became part of every day life, however tiresome and absurd their effects were from time to time.

In May 1971 there was a change of leadership in the GDR. Erich Honecker followed the ageing Ulbricht as leader of the SED. It was the "architect of the Wall" who, of all people, was now pulling the strings. However, many people in the GDR saw new hope in this change of leadership and their optimism actually seemed to be partly well-founded during the period of détente which brought noticeable improvements in terms of travel and visits. In 1974 both German States opened "permanent representations" (instead of embassies) in East Berlin or Bonn and the GDR gained increasing recognition internationally. In the years that followed, however, there was no obvious improvement in living standards or political or social liberalisation not to mention any relaxation of the border regime. Quite the opposite – the border installations were further strengthened. Right up until 1989 there were always people who were prepare to risk their lives because they simply weren't able to stand the restrictions that the GDR imposed on them. From 1985/86 the Border Troops even recorded a substantial increase in the number of attempted and successful escape operations – in some sections of the Wall by as much as 20%.

From East to West, from West to East

On 21st August 1988 at about 10 a.m, dozens of tourists on the banks of the Spree by the Reichstag, watched in total amazement as four young people, two women and two men, fought their through the border installations. They had almost reached the east bank of the Spree when a border guard spotted them. They dived headfirst into the water and then tried to swim towards the west bank. GDR border guards followed the desperate fugitives in a boat and grabbed hold of one of the women who managed to pull herself free. A camera team, which happened to be on the west side of the Spree, filmed the dramatic scenes and with the encouragement of the onlookers, all four fugitives finally reached the west bank, totally exhausted.

This escape, which was filmed live and watched by spectators who were at first horrified and then jubilant, gave the Border Troop Command serious problems. Above all "the political motivation for border duty is not yet sufficiently effective." So a new instruction went out: "To reassess units for their effectiveness with the public and appoint carefully selected border guards and where necessary, promote them to 3 AGT (members of the Border Troops)"[35].

However, the effect of these measures was not as desired. A few months later on 14th February 1989, two men succeeded in escaping at roughly the same place. They broke through the border fences with a lorry and then jumped into the Spree wearing wetsuits to protect them from the cold. They just about managed to get to the west bank but a third fugitive was picked up by a Border Troop boat.

There were also "border breakthroughs" from West to East. In the seventies, for example, a West Berliner climbed over the Wall in Kreuzberg five times and was regularly arrested. When the Border Troop Officer interrogated him as to why he didn't use the border crossing point he answered unflinchingly that he lived in Kreuzberg right opposite his friends and that this was the most direct route and therefore the quickest. The border guards had no answer to this logic and the "border violator" was sent back to West Berlin – until the next time.

To such "wall jumpers" the Wall was a personal irritation or even "a physical challenge". For instance at the beginning of the seventies Rainer W., aged 18, got over the border installations near Potsdam-Babelsberg to the West for the first time. But he only stayed for a weekend because he "didn't really like it too much". A few months after returning to the East he climbed over the Wall again, driven by an inner urge. Eventually W. had permission from the GDR authorities to settle in West Berlin – but he jumped over again, this time from West to East. On each occasion, after a short interrogation the Border Troops got rid of this tiresome "Wall jumper" by sending him back to West Berlin.

Whilst politicians from the West painstakingly struggled in their negotiations to make the Wall less impenetrable, some of their more rebellious contemporaries declared their own personal war on the monstrosity. One of the most comical phenomena of this "scene" was without doubt the American, John Runnings, who launched several attacks on the Wall in 1986/87. He came to Berlin in the summer of 1986 and using a ladder climbed over the Wall from the West. Neither West Berlin policemen nor GDR border soldiers could stop him from carrying out a balancing act for about 500 metres

along the top of the Wall, watched by numerous spectators who were clapping and encouraging him. Finally the DDR guards forced him to come down and took him into custody. However, in order to avoid further embarrassment and diplomatic complications, the authorities sent him back after a short interrogation.

Runnings was not to be intimidated and a few days later he started a new campaign where he sat astride the Wall and hit it symbolically with a hammer. He was immediately arrested by GDR border guards and sent back to West Berlin the next day. His third "Wall adventure" cost him a 53 hour stay in a GDR prison.

On the morning of 1st July 1988 the border guards in the area around Potsdamer Platz were presented with a very unusual challenge – a "mass escape" to the East. Over 200 West Berlin punks, inhabitants of a commune on the so-called Lenné triangle, were fleeing from the police, who were closing in on them, over the Wall into East Berlin. This was the end of a spectacle which had lasted for several months and which became one of the more amusing incidents at the Wall. The incident was all due to one of the topographical peculiarities which led to some bizarre situations at various places on the border. The Wall by no means stood on the exact demarcation line between East and West Berlin but was usually about one or two metres into East Berlin and at some places considerably further. In the middle of the city on Potsdamer Platz there was a site of about four hectares between Lenné, Bellevue and Ebert streets, which belonged to East Berlin but which lay outside the Wall.

In March 1988 East Berlin and the West Berlin Senate agreed on an exchange of territory which meant that the Lenné triangle would belong to the West. However, until this agreement came in to force on 1st July 1988 the area remained outside their terri-

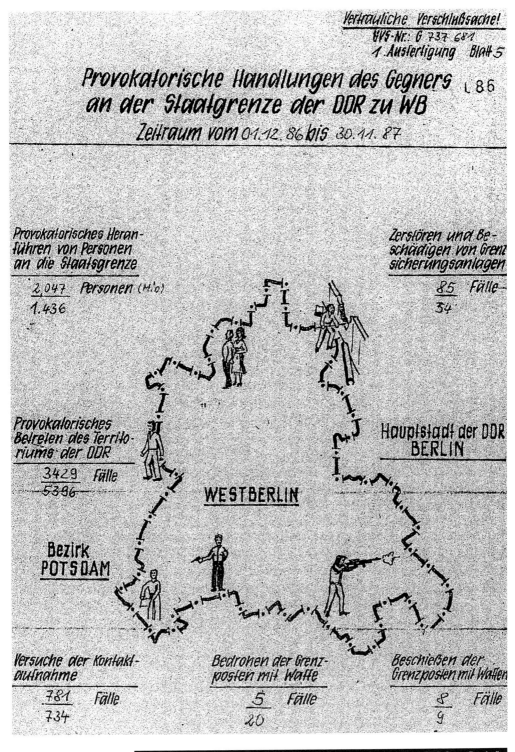

Border Troop illustration of protest actions and other incidents at the "GDR State Border".

tory. This situation was exploited by some Kreuzberg youths from the "alternative scene" who erected a commune there in order to protest about the Senate's building plans. Over the following weeks, the Berliners watched with growing amusement as the squatters played a game of cat and mouse with the West Berlin custodians of the law. Every time there was a scrap the youths moved back into the Lenné triangle to where the West Berlin Police could not follow them.

As soon as the exchange of territory came into force, 900 police immediately closed in and put an end to the "to-ing and fro-ing" by using tear gas. Over 200 squatters escaped arrest by jumping over the Wall. This action was not entirely a surprise to the GDR Border Troops and they reacted calmly to this unusual "Wall breakthrough". The punks were put on lorries and driven to some barracks, given breakfast and after their details were taken they were sent back to West Berlin through various border crossing points.

A white surface invites decoration. This was the feeling of many West Berliners when "Border Wall 75" was erected in 1976, a plain surface of concrete slabs 3.60 metres high and several kilometres long, crying out to be painted and written on. But at no point did the Wall mark the border; it was on East Berlin territory and the distance to the actual border was at least one metre. This meant that for graffiti artists the creative possibilities generously offered by the West side of the Wall were also an invitation to permanently "violate" the border. This is also the way the GDR Border Troops viewed the situation and for years border soldiers were sent through the small openings in the Wall with a paintbrush and bucket to paint over the graffiti.

In 1984 Rainer Hildebrandt, Director of the "Haus am Checkpoint Charlie" in West-Berlin had the idea of launching a Wall painting competition which had the slogan "Overcoming the Wall by painting it" and many renowned international artists, including Lew Nussberg, Christophe Bouchets, Richard Hambleton and Jonathan Borowsky, took part. Later the graffiti star, Keith Haring painted the Wall with his famous male figures. In the meantime the Border Troops had more or less given up removing the paintings on the "enemy" side of the Wall except in one or two exceptional cases.

Although people had generally got used to the Wall there were still events which caused the West Berliners' emotions to rise. One such instance was in May 1975 when five-year old Cetin from Kreuzberg fell into the Spree when he was playing. Some West Berlin divers arrived within a few minutes but were not allowed into the water and had to watch helplessly as the boy drowned, because at this point the whole breadth of the Spree belonged to East Berlin. A GDR border boat arrived too late at the scene of the accident and could only recover the Turkish boy's body from the water.

This incident released a storm of anger and indignation. Hundreds of people gathered on the Kreuzberg bank of the Spree and held up banners accusing the SED regime of "Child murder" and "Inhumanity".

These kinds of events, which brought the Wall sharply into the public consciousness, did not fit into the GDR's plans. After the boy's death East and West came to an agreement about "unbureaucratic" emergency help with "accidents at the border".

Right by the border: enclaves and idyllic retreats

The Lenné triangle was only one of the places where the course of the Wall led to comical results in the division of the city. There was also the West Berlin enclave of

Steinstücken. This 13-hectare area with its 130 inhabitants in the south-east of the city was surrounded by GDR territory. Since the end of the war its only connection with West Berlin consisted of a 1.1 kilometre track across a field, on which the inhabitants had to pass through two checkpoints. When the Wall was built, Steinstücken was completely cut off from West Berlin and its ability to survive was in question. On 21st September 1961 General Clay, a man known for his fast decision making, flew to Steinstücken at short notice by helicopter to demonstrate that the area belonged to West Berlin. Three US soldiers were stationed in Steinstücken to give it direct "protection".

But for the inhabitants it was the beginning of many years of torment and harassment. Only officially registered inhabitants of the enclave and the fire brigade, doctors or midwives were allowed past the border barriers until the Four Powers Agreement was signed. Then, in August 1972, there was an exchange of territory which opened a direct road connection between Steinstücken and West Berlin, enclosed on both sides by a 3.6 metre high Wall.

Another enclave was the so-called Eiskeller (ice cellar), which was connected with the West Berlin borough of Spandau by a no-through road.

While the Wall sometimes left out large areas, such as the Lenné triangle, at other places bizarre building measures were undertaken in order to wall in plots of land and houses. This was the case with the "Entenschnabel" (duck's beak) in Hermsdorf in North Berlin where a neatly walled-in strip of territory projected into West Berlin. At some places, as in Treptow the East and West Berlin garden allotment colonies were so close together that people could see each other's vegetable beds – but they couldn't enjoy a cup of coffee together.

Elsewhere an allotment grew up at Mariannenplatz in Kreuzberg. In 1986 a 60-year old Turkish man and his wife moved to an

Western attempts at the Wall to influence the GDR authorities and register protests, as here in 1967, were recorded on camera by the GDR Border Troops and carefully stored in the archives.

area right next to Wall and when he asked who owned a disused plot of land there, he was given the answer "nobody". So Osman Kalin decided straightaway to plant a vegetable garden there, although the plot lay on East Berlin territory. Here, as well, the Wall had left out a fairly large area which was accessible to the West. To begin with, the GDR border guards wanted to drive the Turk off the land and even threatened to shoot him. But Kalin and his wife weren't intimidated and carried on growing their vegetables. In the end the Border Regiment let the matter drop.

Youth protests in East Berlin

"The Wall must go!" It took a fair amount of courage to voice this demand in 1977 on Alexanderplatz in East Berlin, and all the more so because the date was 7th October, the official anniversary of the founding of the GDR. In the centre of East Berlin 28 years of the "Workers and Farmers State" was being celebrated with a programme of music and dance, including organised cheer-

ing. The first scuffles between some youths and the People's Police broke out at a jazz concert; there were stones thrown and some shop windows were smashed. A real street fight developed from practically nothing and the uniformed forces sent in reacted with considerable violence. About 1,000 young people hit back at them with jeering and chanting slogans of hatred including "The Wall must go!" over and over again. Three youths lost their lives in these violent riots and several dozen people suffered serious injuries. Over 150 arrests were made by the police and Stasi riot squads.

It was the first time that there had been a mass protest in East Berlin against the Wall. It was almost as if there had been a clash between two worlds: on one side the "cheering workers" and on the other hundreds of young people who only needed one small spark to ignite their anger against the SED regime and the symbol of its rule.

In 1987 music led to more mass protests against the Wall, which again resulted in serious violence breaking out between

Even photos of such "provocative enemy actions" landed up in the Border Troop archives.

youths and the police. Between 6th and 9th June 1987 the international pop stars, David Bowie, Genesis and Eurythmics held a series of widely-acclaimed concerts at the Reichstag Building. Some of the loudspeakers were turned towards the East where about 4,000 young people were standing on Unter den Linden, so that they could at least participate acoustically in the Rock spectacle. The area around the Brandenburg Gate had largely been sealed off by Border Troops and members of the Stasi. However, during the early hours of 9th June several hundred youths had managed to break through the barriers and get nearer to the Brandenburg Gate. A large street battle developed between the Rock fans and the police, the Border Troops and the Stasi. Chants of "The Wall must go!" and "Gorbachev, Gorbachev" could be heard far and wide. The crowd was eventually dispersed with the use of truncheons and the Stasi and police made 200 arrests.

In the mid-eighties the border installations in the area of Brandenburg Gate/Pariser Platz were reinforced. The Director of the "Information Centre at the Brandenburg Gate", Lieutenant Colonel Ganßauge, explained this action as follows: "With the present system it is possible to crawl under the barrier and get into the street area in the Border Zone or to provoke the border guards. This area provides a convenient site for demonstrations, especially when foreign Party and State delegations are making official visits."[36]

This was supposed to be prevented by the erection of further metal railings and fitting additional remote-controlled gates. The required building works were undertaken under strict control by the Border Troops in Summer 1984.

It so happened that in the mid-eighties the two most powerful men in the world came to visit the Wall fairly soon after one another. Whilst in 1986 the Soviet Leader Gorbachev was still dutifully expressing his gratitude to the "heroic Border Troops" for their service in the security of Europe, in June 1987 US President Ronald Reagan was directing these words from the Brandenburg Gate to the new Kremlin chief: "…as long as the Gate is shut, this Wall will continue to stand as a scar: it is not just the German question which remains open but the question of freedom for the whole of humanity … General Secretary Gorbachev, if you strive for peace, if you want the Soviet Union and Eastern Europe to be wealthy, if you want liberalisation, then come here to this gate. Mr Gorbachev, open this gate! Mr Gorbachev, pull down this Wall!"

The GDR Border Troop put up huge loud speakers at the Brandenburg Gate to drown Reagan's speech, which was aimed directly at the East Berlin population, with music. In the West the US President was somewhat ridiculed for this speech, if not treated with hostility. This was perhaps indicative of the widespread indifference to the Wall, which according to popular opinion would still be standing for years to come.

High Tech Wall 2000

The Wall "will still be standing in 50 or 100 years if the reasons for its existence are not removed".[37] These words of Party and State leader, Honecker, on 19th January 1989 must have made many people in the GDR shake all over. In 1989, although Gorbachev had already introduced far-reaching liberalisation in the Soviet Union, the Border Troop leadership still saw no reason to consider relaxing the border regime. On the contrary, with express reference to Honecker's declaration of a "100 year Wall", an extension of the border installations was planned for beyond the year 2000. "The situation remains that … in the coming years (up to 2000 and beyond) the GDR must continue through its Border Troops to reinforce the security regime on the border with the Federal Republic and with Berlin (West)."[38]

The GDR planned things well ahead. In 1988/89, for example, detailed "future plans" for improving the Wall were drawn up, where two targets could be followed simultaneously. On the one hand the border was supposed to be made more difficult for fugitives to cross and on the other hand the SED leadership was concerned that there was as little shooting as possible at the Wall. Every shot, every death at the border damaged the international reputation of the GDR and this credibility was of increasing importance during a period of a rapidly rising requirement for credit.

The result of these efforts was the project "High Tech Wall 2000", a border where any escape attempts were already electronically monitored well before the actual Wall itself and foiled, if possible, without the use of weapons. The announcement made by the Border Troop Command reads as follows:

Geplante Maßnahmen für 1989

Bezeichnung der Grenzsicherungsanlage	Ausbaustand 31. 12. 1988	geplant 1989 im Abschnitt Hptst. d. DDR BERLIN	Bezirk POTSDAM
Grenzmauer	103 km	1,1 km	0,9 km
Grenzzaun	70 km	1,0 km	13,8 km
Grenzsignal-u. Sperrzaun	27 km	-	7,5 km
Beobachtungsturm (BT-9)	111 Stück	2 Stück	6 Stück

"Above all such proven physical effects and technical means should be used to reduce under a system of high security the starting points for provocation by the enemy against the GDR."[39] In other words "High Tech" instead of shooting.

Both aims, the prevention of further "border breakthroughs" and the least use of weapons possible, could be also found in the Border Troop Command plan of 6th May 1988 on the "Development of border security technology for the period 1990–2000".

Overall there was an increased reliance on sensor technology and electronics instead of barriers, walls and guns. A whole range of technical innovations was envisaged. "New effective supplementary equipment for the electrified fencing, especially for the signalling of climbing over" were to be installed. The technical, material and logistic means had to be created to put in place the blanket-coverage micro-electronic sensor technology, to collect the digitalized data centrally and to evaluate it with the aid of computers, all within the required time frame. At the same time there were plans to equip the border patrols with mobile movement detectors and night vision aids.

The GDR Defence Ministry awarded numerous development contracts, for example to the "Central Institute for Earth Physics", in Potsdam for "Seismic reporting systems". In January 1985 the Potsdam physicists introduced their prototypes: "Detection: a single person at 3–8 metres, a lorry at 40–100 metres." The cost of installation was 15,000 marks per kilometre. But there were problems: "The ability to differentiate between humans and animals with the help of seismic sensors has not yet been achieved."[40] The "High Tech Wall" project was soon throwing up even bigger difficulties which were caused by the backwardness of the electronic industry and the notorious shortage of finances in the GDR. Thus in June 1988 the Chief of Planning in the Ministry

"It will still remain, even in 100 years time..." Projections by the Border Troops in 1989.

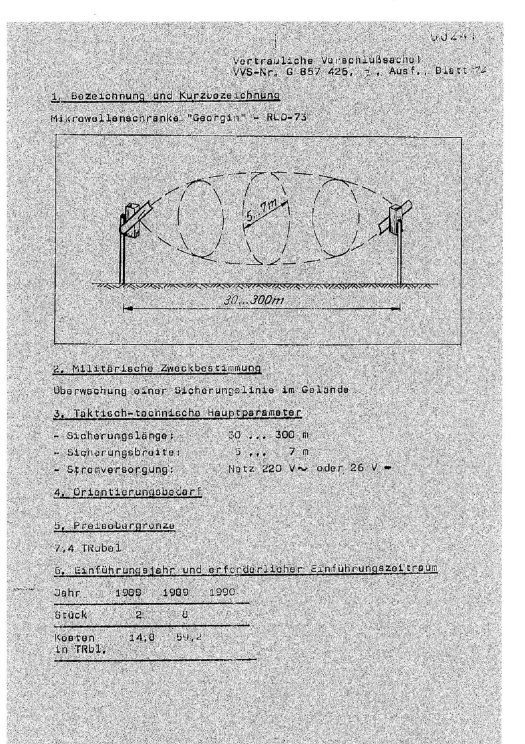

ปป 241

Vertrauliche Verschlußsache!
VVS-Nr. G 857 426, ः., Ausf., Blatt 74

1. Bezeichnung und Kurzbezeichnung

Mikrowellenschranke "Georgin" - RLD-73

2. Militärische Zweckbestimmung

Überwachung einer Sicherungslinie im Gelände

3. Taktisch-technische Hauptparameter

- Sicherungslänge: 30 ... 300 m
- Sicherungsbreite: 5 ...   7 m
- Stromversorgung: Netz 220 V~ oder 26 V –

4. Orientierungsbedarf

5. Preisobergrenze

7,4 TRubel

6. Einführungsjahr und erforderlicher Einführungszeitraum

Jahr	1988	1989	1990
Stück	2	8	
Kosten in TRbl.	14,8	59,2	

The plan for a "High-Tech Border" included this "Georgin" barrier fitted with microwave beams and sensors.

of Defence complained that: "Sensors to pick up the magnetic, infra-red and acoustic fields of individuals ... which work reliably in heavily populated and overgrown areas, do not yet exist."[41]

Even in 1988 and 1989 the plans to reinforce and extend the border regime were pursued with vigour, despite the increasing economic and political crisis in the GDR. A proposal by the "Chief of Technology and Weapons" of the Border Troops contained a whole catalogue of electronic innovations for the "State Border with Berlin (West)". The crucial item was the "electrified border fence 90" with "metal sensors, field sensors, energy supply equipment, security border signal fence gate and water duct " linked to a computer-aided "central analysis equipment". An electronic "surveillance machine GÜG 89" was to be installed from 1993 onwards which was estimated to cost 1.2 million marks per 100 machines on the inner-German border. Anyone approaching the fences or the Wall would be detected by an infra-red barrier (at a cost of 15,000 marks each). From 1991 the "Vibrations detector "Gavott" DS-80 W" would be installed specifically to guard water barriers. The cost per system: 15,500 roubles. The function of the "Radar detection equipment "Kredo" –

1 RL133" was described as follows: "Surveillance of a section of ground when entered by persons, or driven on by wheeled or tracked vehicles." Cost: 30,000 roubles each. In 1988/99 the introduction of a "microwave barrier" with the description "Georgin-RLD-73" was already planned for the surveillance of a section of ground.[42]

The financing of the High Tech Border was a delicate subject. In June 1988 a communication from the Defence Ministry went out to the Border Troop Command in which the problem of finance was particularly emphasised. With the development and installation of "modern security arrangements there are high material and financial costs involved. Particular attention must be paid to the economic aspects of working out the main trends for the time span 1991–1995/ 2000."[43] This appeal for economy is understandable if the catastrophic situation economic situation of the GDR was taken into account, which in 1988 was in a state of insolvency. The 1989 GDR budget, however, still contained expenditure of 1,221 billion marks for border security. Until 1996 alone 42.2 million marks were to be spent on "border installation 90 'GSA 90' ".

But history, or rather the people of the GDR, had other ideas.

THE FALL OF THE WALL

A system breaks up

On the East side of the "Iron Curtain" things had begun to ferment. From the mid-eighties criticism of the Communist Party was particularly loud in Poland and Hungary. Opposition groups became more and more popular and were increasingly courageous in their protest against political oppression. Since March 1985 Mikhail Gorbachev was the leading light of the Communist Party in the Soviet Union.

He made the concepts of "Glasnost" and "Perestroika" famous throughout the world. But in East Berlin it was still the same old men in power. Member of the Politbüro, Kurt Hager, said of the political changes in the Soviet Union: If your neighbour renovates his home, then you must start to wallpaper your own room. But the Party and State leadership of the GDR saw no need for action. In spring 1989 the political and economic crisis of the East Block countries came to a dramatic head. Hungary and Poland were the first States to withdraw from the obvious failure of the "real existing Socialism" by introducing a multi-party system and a market economy. In addition, the Hungarian reformers were no longer prepared to take participate in what was the imprisonment of the East European population. On 2nd May 1989 the barbed wire fences on the border with Austria were cut. The "Iron Curtain" and with it the Wall, had been torn for the first time.

In the ensuing weeks and months the border between Hungary and Austria became a loop-hole for an increasing number of GDR citizens. On 19th August the first mass exodus of GDR citizens since the building of the wall took place near Sopron. Over 600 people crossed over the border into Austria during what almost amounted to a political event. The West German Embassies in Budapest and Prague turned into veritable army camps in the late summer to accommodate the GDR citizens who wanted to leave their country. On 11th September the Hungarian Government declared their border with Austria officially open. The GDR leadership was up to its neck in water. Every Monday since mid-September every Monday there were demonstrations in Leipzig for political reforms and from week to week the number of demonstrators was increasing. At the same time the Soviet leadership was indicating that the stabilisation of the GDR could not happen at the expense of the interests in Moscow in relation to West Germany and Western Europe. "Life will punish those who come too late", declared Mikhail Gorbachev.

At the beginning of 1989, when the last SED leaders realised that only credit from the West could rescue the GDR economically (and thereby politically), appropriate action was also taken with regard to the border regime. Nothing had damaged the international reputation of the GDR since 1961 as much as the shootings at the Wall. A command went out from the Defence Minister on 3rd April 1989 that no shots were to be fired to stop border breakthroughs except in self-defence or if the life of another person, for example a hostage, was being threatened.

Only two months previously, in the night of the 5th/6th February 1989, 20-year old Chris Gueffroy had been killed in an escape attempt in Berlin-Treptow. Gueffroy was the last fugitive who lost his life at the Wall. But shots were still fired even after the order of

3rd April 1989 when two East Berlin youths tried to sprint through the border crossing point at Chausseestraße on 8th April and were stopped by warning shots from a GDR passport controller and subsequently arrested.

9th November 1989

History has never been made or proclaimed quite so casually. On the evening of 9th November, Günter Schabowski, member of the Politbüro, held a press conference in the International Press Centre in Mohrenstraße in East Berlin, which was broadcast live on GDR television. There was a sense of tense expectation among the journalists from all over the world because the events of the previous days had come to a dramatic climax. Only that morning the whole Politbüro of the SED had resigned. But still an exhausted Schabowski started to give scanty reports of the last Central Committee meeting.

At 18.53, at the request of an Italian journalist, Schabowski rummaged about for a piece of paper and read it quickly, stumbling several times. It was obvious that he didn't know what was on the piece of paper, which had been handed to him shortly before the conference by Egon Krenz, Honecker's successor. "Private journeys abroad can be applied for without presenting conditions, reasons for travel or names of relatives. Permission will be granted at short notice. The responsible departments of the passport and registration authorities of the VPKÄ" – Schabowski looked up – "of the People's Police authorities in the GDR, are instructed to distribute visas for permanent exit at once, without having to present valid reasons for permanent exit."

A murmur went through the room. What was it supposed to mean? "Private journeys", "reasons for travel", "permission at short notice"? There was confusion among the journalists. Even Günter Schabowski on the podium obviously had trouble understanding what he had read.

Question: "Does it apply to West Berlin?"

Schabowski shrugged his shoulders and rummaged in his papers: "Well (pause) – yes, yes." Then he continued reading: "The permanent exit is valid at all crossing point of the GDR into the Federal Republic or West Berlin."

Question: "When does it come into force?"

Once again Schabowski rummaged helplessly amongst his papers: "Well, as far as I can see, ... straightaway, immediately."[44]

The main item in the "Tagesschau" (TV Evening News in the West, ed.) at 8 p.m. was, "GDR opens its border!" Many East Germans heard what Schabowski had to say. What happened next on 9th November 1989 in Berlin was a result of many things: the hopes and desires of the people, the interpretation and speculation of the media, the insecurity of the SED leadership and the helplessness of a border regime without any orders.

It was an historic moment in which suppositions quickly became facts, misunderstandings became information and in which, above all, the bitterness and the hopes of the East Berliners became deeds and the wishes for freedom became a reality.

At 8.30 p.m., jolted into action by the news on the radio and television, several hundred people had already gathered at the Bornholmerstraße border crossing point. Some of them were demanding the border guards to let them through, others had just come "to see what was going on". The crowd was growing by the minute. More and more East Berliners were streaming towards the crossing points at Invalidenstraße and Sonnenallee. The number of people who wanted to watch developments with their own eyes was also growing on the West Berlin side.

The pressure on the border barriers was increasing. The Commanders and border guards were nervous and unsure what to do. No-one had told them how they had to behave. At about 9 p.m. the crowd at Bornholmer Straße vociferously demanded the border to be opened – there was a tailback of cars for over a kilometre.

Continually growing in numbers, they were chanting, "Open the Gate! Open the Gate!" with increasing fervour. At 10.30 p.m. the Officer in charge of the border crossing point at Bornholmer Straße said to his superior: "We can't hold them back any longer. We must open the barrier. I'll switch off the controls and let the people out."[45]

Thousands of people now streamed over Bornholmer Bridge towards West Berlin. Shortly afterwards the barriers fell in Sonnenallee and Invalidenstraße under the onslaught of people.

One man was wearing pyjamas under his coat. "We live in Bornholmer Straße, in the East ... I was indoors, the wife went down with the dog and came up again and said: Hey, you, they're all going to the West! I wasn't even dressed, but over I came."

Several hundred people had gathered on both sides of Checkpoint Charlie, for 28 years the scene of so many dramatic events and direct confrontations. As the pressure increased on the barriers both from East and West, the GÜST Commandant resorted to a defensive measure. At 11 p.m. he had all available barriers and metal shuttered doors closed. Hundreds of West Berliners were shouting "Let us in!" and from East Berlin came "Let us out!" Just before midnight the Commandant gave in to the pressure and the barriers were raised at Checkpoint Charlie as well.

At two minutes past midnight the East Berlin police announced that all border crossing points in the city had been opened. The Wall had fallen.

Most East Berliners were completely overwhelmed by the fall of the Wall and their newly acquired freedom. They pushed their way through the barriers cheering, many with tears in their eyes and were given an enthusiastic welcome by the West Berliners. People who had never set eyes on each other before were embracing. Trabis and Wartburgs were moving bumper to bumper through the stream of cheering people towards West Berlin. People did not know how to put their feelings into words. "Crazy!" was the word heard most often that night. One Trabi driver wound down his window in joyful exuberance: "I keep

Günter Schabowski (right) at the historic press conference on the evening of 9th November 1989.

2

B e s c h l u ß v o r s c h l a g

Zur Veränderung der Situation der ständigen Ausreise von
DDR-Bürgern nach der BRD über die CSSR wird festgelegt:

1. Die Verordnung vom 30. November 1988 über Reisen von
   Bürgern der DDR in das Ausland (GBl. I Nr. 25 S. 271)
   findet bis zur Inkraftsetzung des neuen Reisegesetzes
   keine Anwendung mehr.

2. Ab sofort treten folgende ~~zeitweilige Übergangs~~regelungen
   für Reisen und ständige Ausreisen aus der DDR in das
   Ausland in Kraft:

   a) Privatreisen nach dem Ausland können ohne Vorliegen von Vor-
      aussetzungen (Reiseanlässe und Verwandtschaftsverhältnisse)
      beantragt werden. Die Genehmigungen werden kurzfristig er-
      teilt. Versagungsgründe werden nur in besonderen Ausnahme-
      fällen angewandt.

   b) Die zuständigen Abteilungen Paß- und Meldewesen der VPKÄ
      in der DDR sind angewiesen, Visa zur ständigen Ausreise
      unverzüglich zu erteilen, ohne daß dafür noch geltende Vor-
      aussetzungen für eine ständige Ausreise vorliegen müssen.
      Die Antragstellung auf ständige Ausreise ist wie bisher auch
      bei den Abteilungen Innere Angelegenheiten möglich.

   c) Ständige Ausreisen können über alle Grenzübergangsstellen
      der DDR zur BRD bzw. zu Berlin (West) erfolgen.

   d) Damit entfällt die vorübergehend ermöglichte Erteilung von
      entsprechenden Genehmigungen in Auslandsvertretungen der
      DDR bzw. die ständige Ausreise mit dem Personalausweis der
      DDR über Drittstaaten.

3. Über die zeitweiligen Übergangsregelungen ist die
   beigefügte Pressemitteilung am (10. November 1989)
   zu veröffentlichen.

   Verantwortlich: Regierungssprecher beim Ministerrat
                   der DDR

The piece of paper mistakenly read out by Schabowski, which led to the fall of the Wall on 9th November.

pinching myself. I'm taking the old crate down the Kurfürstendamm." Champagne was flowing at the crossing points. Practically the whole population of Berlin was up and celebrating.

The Border Troops of the GDR were totally unprepared for the fast and furious events of the evening of 9th November 1989. The travel regulations announced by Schabowski and the ensuing developments had come as a complete surprise to both commanders and troops.

On the evening of 9th November, Border Troop Commandant, Baumgarten, received the news of the worsening situation at the border crossing points in the Defence Ministry in Strausberg where he had gone after a meeting of the Central Committee. He was so totally surprised by events that he was incapable of giving any concrete instructions. The leaders of the Army and the Border Troops had manifestly lost all control of the situation. They parted at 1.a.m. without making any decisions. Chief of Staff of the Border Troops, Major General Dieter Teichmann, later complained bitterly about a lack of information: "That's why we had no chance to make any necessary preparations at the border ... at first I just couldn't grasp the fact that I had heard about the opening of the border on television."[46]

The GÜST Commanders each made their own decision about not using force to hold back people pushing forward from the East. It was quite clear to all of them that, in the words of the Border Troop Duty Officer at Bornholmer Straße: "If the masses ran towards us and we opened fire, then we would be the ones with our necks in the noose."[47]

A considerable number of members of the Border Troops felt angry and disappointed and they made no secret of this fact. A Protest Resolution lodged by Border Regiment 36 on 10th November 1989 stated: "We view the events of 9.11.1989 and 10.11.1989 as treachery and mockery of the achievements of the instruments of protection and security, especially the Border Troops. Decisions were made without informing us and which forced us to abandon all our military and political principles."

Many Border Troop Officers later expressed their disappointment at how quickly the political leaders of the GDR "disappeared from the scene": "On 7th October they were still convinced that the Wall would stand for another hundred years, in spite of the fact that on this 40th Anniversary of the GDR slogans had appeared on the houses saying that the people weren't behind them any more. ... Yes, and then the border was suddenly open and those politicians, for whom we had guarded it over the years, had vanished into oblivion."[48]

The morale of many members of the Border Troops had unmistakably suffered seriously in the previous months and weeks, despite what the tenor of Border Regiment 36's Protest Resolution might suggest. More and more border soldiers and officers could not see much sense in the "reliable protection of the border". There was a growing need for discussion within the Border Regiments, but at command level the only reaction to everything was silence.

On 10th November – the "night of nights" was over, and the whole of Berlin was still in a mood of great celebration – Party Leader Krenz and Defence Minister Keßler ordered military precautions. An "operative leadership group" was formed whose task was to assemble current information about the situation at the open borders, to assess the "situation of the opponent" and to prepare "proposals for decisions for the leadership of the whole State." However, it was very unclear in what direction these decisions should go and what they should prevent. What was evident was the efforts of the GDR leadership to stop the individual centres of power (Party, State, Army, Border Troops, State Security) from drifting uncontrollably apart and to seize the initiative again. There were also mobilisation measures which, however, were not far-reaching and were not based on sending the military in to close the border again. Afterwards, Deputy Defence Minister Fritz Streletz, among others, stressed the fact that such a possibility was never considered after 9th November. In fact, in the early hours of 10th November, orders were given for the 1st Mot. (motorised) Rifle Division in Potsdam (about 10,000 men, three Tank Regiments, one Artillery Regiment, one Anti-Rocket Regiment) and the Airborne Regiment 40 (600 men) stationed in Lehnin, to be prepared for battle.

Since 10th November at 2 a.m., shortly after the Wall had fallen, the whole of Central Border Command (11,500 men) had been raised to a fully operational level. The NVA directive to seize "measures for strengthening border security and raising battle readiness to an operation level capable of securing the border and fulfilling battle and mobilisation tasks" was in force.[49] This included the distribution of munitions and the activation of weapons and vehicles. The Ministry of State Security was also placed on high alert. With immediate effect all available officials were commanded "in view of the situation … to remain with service or operational units until the order is withdrawn".[50] A total of 30,000 men were fully operational.

The story of a piece of paper

It is indisputable that in the light of the explosive atmosphere among the population and the growing pressure on the streets – the Leipzig "Monday Demonstrations" and the mass demonstrations in East Berlin on 4th November – the GDR leadership had seen no alternative but to liberalise travel condi-

tions, which in effect meant opening the border. However, this was supposed to happen under the strict control of the regime, according to a planned time-scale and fully safeguarded by GDR State sovereignty. In addition, the CSSR, which had had to cope for weeks with an enormous flood of refugees, had put the SED leadership on the spot.

After hectic and partly confused discussions within the leadership committees of Party and State, the Ministry of State Security was given the task of preparing a new law on travel regulations. On 7th November Lieutenant General Gerhard Neiber, Deputy to the Stasi Leader Mielke, submitted a proposal according to which "permanent exits" (i.e. moving to the Federal Republic, ed.) should be granted by issuing a visa, "without having to provide valid reasons." On the morning of 9th November four senior officers, two from the Ministry of State Security and two from the Ministry of the Interior, sat down together to work out a new travel law. They agreed to "do the job properly" which meant combining the questions of "permanent exit" and "personal travel". This was intended to prevent people making short trips and visits from being at a disadvantage in comparison with "emigrants". The four officers felt that if such people had to go through bureaucratic hurdles this would lead to further unrest among the GDR population at large. At the time only 4 million people (out of a total population of 17 million) were in possession of a passport and this was now to be a general requirement. In this way they thought they could put a stop to a sudden mass uprising. The Ministry of State Security accepted the plan with a waiting period until publication until 4 a.m. on 10th November.

Meanwhile the political situation was becoming more and more tense. On the previous day, 8th November the whole Politbüro had resigned. The old guard around

Mielke, Hager, Axen and Stoph stepped down. Egon Krenz had already replaced Honecker as General Secretary on 18th October. People like Schabowski and Kleiber came forward.

When the proposal for permanent exit and temporary visits, which ran contrary to the original brief, was submitted to the newly constituted Politbüro, Schabowski was not present. At about 5.30 p.m. Krenz pressed Schabowksi in his new function as "Government Spokesman" to announce the new ruling straightaway. Schabowski, however was unaware that it was still formally only a cabinet "proposal" and not a "resolution". At about 6 p.m. he stood up in front of the press and matters took their course.

The end of the border regime

With the fall of the Wall on the November 1989 the population of the GDR had to some extent "single-handedly" ended the border regime. The SED leadership and the Border Troop Command had no other alternative but to deal with the practical consequences during the weeks and months that followed. It wasn't easy for the military to get used to the new circumstances. In the Defence Ministry Order 101/89 of 21st December there is still mention of "border violators". "... People who have violated the border must be arrested." However, use of weapons was expressly forbidden except in emergency situations. Basically the top military were perfectly aware that the hour had come. "The engineering and signalling works to reinforce and extend the border are to be stopped ... Border security installations which are no longer required or which will damage the standing of the GDR are to be removed." At the same time the order to shoot was finally abolished. "The use of weapons, with the exception of defending attacks of the lives of members of the Bor-

der Troops or other citizens of the GDR is certainly ruled out."[51] At this point reality had long overtaken these kinds of orders.

At the beginning of January 1990 the GDR government under Hans Modrow (SED/PDS) was in charge of a gradual reduction in the size of the Border Troops of about 50% to 25,000 men. Up to mid-March 1990 1,000 officers and 12,000 men were made redundant.

On 26th June 1990, in respect of the Currency and Social Union with the Federal Republic which came into force on 1st July 1990, the new GDR Minister for Disarmament and Defence, Rainer Eppelmann (CDU) stopped all border controls at the inner-German border and in Berlin. 30th

The borders are open. Trabis and cheering crowds at the Bornholmer Brücke crossing point.

June was the last day that a passport had to be shown when travelling from West Berlin to East Berlin or into the surrounding area. On 21st September, two weeks before the GDR was legally joined to the Federal Republic of Germany, Minister Rainer Eppelmann dissolved the Border Troops. A chapter of post-war German history had come to an end.

Improvised border crossing point at the Brandenburg Gate. Identity checks were still being made here in March 1990.

THE DISAPPEARANCE OF THE WALL

Protecting the Wall – and other court cases

On 20th January 1992 the Berlin District Court announced the verdicts in the first "Wall protection case". Four former border soldiers were accused of shooting 20-year old Chris Gueffroy on February 1989 and fatally wounding him. The main accused, Ingo H., was sentenced to 3 ½ years imprisonment, another man accused with him was given a 16 months suspended sentence. In an appeal hearing Ingo H.'s prison sentence was later turned into a suspended sentence. Both the other accused were set free. There was unrest in the courtroom. Most of the spectators thought the verdict was too lenient and expressed their dissatisfaction.

Over 800 people lost their lives at the Wall and the inner-German border and over 900 were wounded. Afterwards it was proved that more than 230 people were killed at the Berlin Wall. Hundreds sustained injuries and thousands were given long prison sentences after their attempt to escape had failed, and suffered from the consequences for many decades to follow. Someone had to be held responsible for all this. But who was responsible and what were they guilty of? The story of the Wall was by no means over on 9th November 1989.

After 1990 the German law courts now faced the difficult task of determining and assess the personal fault of each of the individuals accused – the border guard who fired the shot, as well as the member of the Politbüro who had been part of the original decision making process. Were the "wall protectors" who had acted on orders the "correct" people to be accused? What about the political dictators and military commanders? And there was a basic rule which had to be taken into account: no punishment could be given unless a law had been broken. Only crimes which broke the laws of the GDR could be brought to trial.

Up to the middle of 1999 there were 70 such trials in Berlin, including those against the border soldiers who took part in the shooting of Peter Fechter and Günter Litfin, the first fugitive who was killed. It was the "wall protectors" who were tried first. The charges brought were "attempted or successful manslaughter". In most cases suspended sentences of between one and two years were imposed, because a verdict of "least serious case of manslaughter" was usually returned. After 1990 there were a total of 3,000 preliminary proceedings concerning violent acts at the Wall and the inner-German border. Charges have been preferred in a mere 200 cases so far.

The first trial against former GDR politicians began in November 1992. The Chairman of the Council of State Erich Honecker, the former Stasi leader Erich Mielke, the former Prime Minister Willi Stoph, and the former Defence Minister Heinz Keßler and his Deputy Fritz Streletz, all members of the National Defence Council of the GDR, had to answer to the courts in Berlin for the fatal shots at the Wall and the inner-German border. It was a long and tortuous trial. Proceedings against three of the accused, Honecker, Stoph and Mielke had to be stopped prematurely for reasons of poor health. The District Court pronounced their verdicts on Keßler, Streletz and Albrecht in September 1993: Prison sentences of between 5 and 7½ years. The court saw the accused not only as "instigators" but also, because of their position of power, as "direct perpetrators".

The accused tried to argue that the GDR border was a military no-go area and that therefore they could not be tried and sentenced according to GDR law, but this strategy did not work. In 1996 in its refusal to accept an application for appeal, the Federal Court stressed that is was not valid if a State "excludes the most serious criminal injustice" as a punishable offence and "… thereby seriously disregards the human rights generally recognised among the international community."[52]

Even Klaus-Dieter Baumgarten, who had been in charge of the Border Troops for many years, and five high-ranking Border Troop Commanders were brought to trial. In September 1996 Baumgarten was sentenced to six years imprisonment for several cases of manslaughter and his deputies were sentenced to three years and three months for their contribution. In March 2000 Baumgarten was granted a repieve. In April 1999 four former Vice-Commanders of the Central Border Command were given suspended sentences for their contribution to manslaughter. A former Commander of the Central Border Command, to which the Berlin Wall belonged, was sentenced to 2½ years imprisonment in August 1999.

Even the members of the last SED Politbüro could not escape criminal prosecution under the law. The court viewed the members of the Politbüro as directly responsible for the fatal shots as the Wall. In August 1997 Egon Krenz was sentenced to 6½ years of imprisonment for six cases of manslaughter (the charge was limited to these six cases for procedural reasons) and those accused with him, Günter Schabowski and Günther Kleiber each received sentences of three years imprisonment. Günter Schabowski was the only one of the accused who during the course of the proceedings admitted to a share of the moral blame.

A Wall trial of another kind, which opened in the Berlin District Court in December 1998, also attracted a lot of interest. Here too the charge was fatal shots at the Berlin Wall; but in this case it concerned a GDR border soldier. After 36 years 61-year old Rudolf M. had to answer to the charge that he had shot and killed GDR guard Reinhold Huhn near Checkpoint Charlie when he was involved in helping some fugitives to escape. In April 1999 M. was given a one year suspended sentence.

Demolition and exploitation

Monte Carlo on a sunny day in June 1990. An illustrious and wealthy crowd from all over the world had gathered in the chic hotel "Metropole Palace", not far from the famous Casino, and was waiting for the start of a very unusual event: The Berlin Wall was coming under the hammer. A total of 81 colourfully painted segments of the Border Wall 75 were auctioned in Monaco on this evening and the lowest price fetched was 50,000 francs.

The well-to-do Italian publisher's wife, Jaguba Rizolli, was able to place her segment of Wall bought at auction for 27,000 marks and produced for 359 GDR marks, in

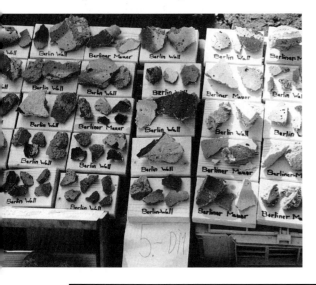

For many months pieces of the Wall were prized souvenirs for tourists from all over the world.

the garden of her villa. A businessman from Zürich bought eleven pieces of the Wall for 1.3 million francs – a good price for bits of painted concrete, which in the freight papers were correctly declared as "builders' rubble". A total of DM 1.8 million was realised at the Monaco event, which according to the organiser, who was seriously billed as "Lelé Berlin Wall Sales Ltd.", were to be used to benefit the reorganisation of the Health Service in the GDR.

From January 1990 segments of the Wall went all over the world, particularly to collectors and enthusiasts, but also to personalities who had helped to earn the victory over the Wall. So US Presidents Ronald Reagan and George Bush each received their own piece of the Wall as did the John F. Kennedy Library in Boston and the CIA, who displayed it in their Headquarters.

"The Wall must go" was the slogan chanted for many years in the battle against the division of Berlin. On 9th November 1989 the time had come to turn this demand into action. At the beginning of 1990 the GDR administration and the municipal authorities of East Berlin decided that the Wall was to be demolished.

There were altogether 106 kilometres of Wall in and around Berlin, 45,000 segments each weighing 2.75 tons had to be removed; plus 127.5 kilometres of electrified and barrier fencing and 302 observation towers.

On 30th November 1990 the last piece of the inner-city Wall on Wedding Provinzstraße was officially carried away. A total length of 32.4 kilometres of Wall and border installations had been removed.

After 29 years it was quite a new feeling: Berlin without a Wall.

The largest part of the Wall was put to good use. A lot of concrete and money changed hands to bring the Wall to the people. To begin with scores of "Wallpeckers" sold the pieces of Wall they had chipped off to Berlin tourists and for several months made a good living out of them.

Most of the concrete segments were broken into little pieces, sold at DM 20 a ton and used mainly for building roads in East Germany.

Disputes about memories

Visitors to Berlin stand helplessly on Potsdamer Platz or in Kochstraße: Where had the Wall actually been?

The dismantling of the Wall and the border installations was an act of external and internal liberation. In the first days and weeks after 9th November there was always applause from bystanders wherever another piece of Wall was being carried away. However, people soon began to object to the thoroughness with which the Wall was being removed from the Berlin street scene. An intense dispute erupted about how the Wall could be preserved in the people's consciousness as a memorial to the victims and a warning for future generations.

There were attempts to keep memories alive. A Wall Memorial and Documentation Centre were opened on Bernauer Straße. The "Haus am Checkpoint Charlie", which stands on the former checkpoint where

Tearing down the segments of the Wall in November 1989.

American and Soviet tanks had faced each other, has preserved some of the installations, including an observation tower. The route of the Wall has been marked out by a 7.5 kilometre line of cobblestones running through the city. But there are only very few places in Berlin where pieces of the Wall have been preserved: at Niederkirchner Straße, at Mühlenstraße in Friedrichshain ("East-Side-Gallery"), and at Bernauer Straße and Leipziger or rather Potsdamer Platz. The Senate pushed ahead with the removal of a piece of "Back-up Wall" at Potsdamer Platz despite numerous public protests.

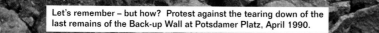

Let's remember – but how? Protest against the tearing down of the last remains of the Back-up Wall at Potsdamer Platz, April 1990.

CHRONOLOGY

1944 12th September
In a statement made in London, the USA, Great Britain and the USSR decide to divide Germany and Berlin into three (later four) Zones of Occupation or Sectors.

1945 5th May
Unconditional surrender of Nazi Germany.

1946 4th December
The Soviet Military administration (SMAD) decrees that the demarcation lines of the Soviet Zone of Occupation should be safeguarded.

1952 26th May
Krushschev Ultimatum: The Soviet Union demands that Berlin has the status of a "free city".

1961 15th June
Ulbricht declares at a press conference in Berlin: "No-one intends to erect a wall".

1961 13th August
The sector borders with West Berlin are closed.

1961 15th August
The first sections of the Wall are erected.

1961 19th August
1500 US soldiers are dispatched to Berlin.

1962 23rd August
A further five of the remaining 12 border crossing points in Berlin are closed. West Berliners are forbidden to enter East Berlin.

1961 24th August
A 24-year old man is shot and killed by a border guard at the Humboldt-Hafen. He is the first fugitive to die at the Berlin Wall.

1961 12th September
Formation of the "Border Troops of the GDR" as part of the NVA ("National People's Army").

1961 27th October
Confrontation between American and Soviet tanks at Checkpoint Charlie.

1962
Installation of the first dog runs.

1962 18th June
The GDR border soldier, Reinhold Huhn, is shot dead by a West German escape helper.

1961 19th June
Border Troops begin to erect a second Wall.

1962 17th August
Peter Fechter is shot during an escape attempt and bleeds to death on the border strip.

1961 21th June
Declaration of an East Berlin "Border Zone" by the Wall, which can only be entered with special permission.

1963 26th June
Visit of President John F. Kennedy to West Berlin.

1963 19th December
The first visitors' permit agreement comes into force; valid until 5th January 1964.

1964 December
The second visitors' permit agreement.

1965 18th December
The third visitors' permit agreement; valid until 2nd January 1966.

1966
Erection of the first observation towers.

1966 7th–20th April and 23rd May–5th June
The fourth visitors' permit agreement.

1966 October
Agreement on the setting up of an office issuing visitors' permits in urgent cases.

1966 December
Breakdown in negotiations about further visitors' permit regulations.

1968
Erection of the "3rd Generation" Wall (concrete segments with a pipe laid on top).

1971
Start of the installation of a "border fence" of barbed wire.

1971 31ˢᵗ January
After a break of 19 years, telephone communications between the two part of Berlin are re-established.

1971 1ˢᵗ February
Re-structuring of the Border Troops; creation of the North, Central and South Border Commands and the Coastal Border Brigade.

1972 3ʳᵈ May
Honecker takes over from Ulbricht as SED Party Leader.

1971 3ʳᵈ September
Signing of the Four Powers Agreement on Berlin.

1971 17ᵗʰ December
Signing of the Transit Agreement between the Federal Republic of Germany and the GDR.

1971 20ᵗʰ December
Signing of an agreement between the West Berlin Senate and the GDR Government to facilitate and improve all travel and visits to East Berlin.

1971 3ʳᵈ June
The Four Powers Agreement comes into force.

1972 21ˢᵗ December
Signing of the Basic Treaty between the Federal Republic and the GDR.

1974 1ˢᵗ January
Border Troops of the GDR are formerly separated from the National Army.

1974
"Back-up Wall" and rear "Border Signal Fence 74" are erected.

1975
Erection of the first observation towers BT9 or BT11, with their angular shape.

1975 29ᵗʰ October
Agreement between the Senate and East Berlin about the rescue measures to be taken in case of accidents at the sector border. Two West Berlin children had drowned in the Spree. Border guards had prevented the West from assisting and had intervened too late themselves.

1976
Erection of the first sections of the "Border Wall 75" ("4ᵗʰ Generation Wall").

1977 7ᵗʰ October
On Alexanderplatz in East Berlin there are serious clashes between youths and police and three youths are fatally wounded. The crowd demands "The Wall must go!"

1980 13ᵗʰ October
Increase in the minimum amount of currency exchange on visits to East Berlin to DM 25. Drastic reduction in the number of visitors.

1981 20ᵗʰ November
Opening of the Teltow Canal for inland water traffic.

1982 25ᵗʰ March
The GDR Parliament passes a new Border Law.

1983 1ˢᵗ July
The National Defence Council of the GDR decides to make further "engineering" improvements to the border installations.

1984
The erection of a border fence fitted with sensors at the "Back-up border".

1987 8ᵗʰ June
During a rock concert at the Reichstag there are clashes in East Berlin between youths and police near the Brandenburg Gate.

1989 19ᵗʰ January
Honecker pronounces in East Berlin that the Wall will "still exist in 100 years time" if the circumstances which led to its erection have not changed.

1989 5ᵗʰ February
20 year old Chris Gueffroy is shot and killed during an escape attempt. He is the last victim of the Wall.

1989 8ᵗʰ April
At the border crossing point of Chausseestraße, an escape attempt by two youths is stopped by a warning shot. These are the last shots fired at the Wall.

1989 4ᵗʰ November
Mass demonstration in East Berlin against the SED Government.

1989 9ᵗʰ November
The border is opened.

1990 30ᵗʰ June
All border controls are stopped.

1989 21ˢᵗ September
The Border Troops of the GDR are disbanded.

NOTES

1 Cf. Petschull, Jürgen, Die Mauer, Hamburg³ 1990, P. 51 ff

2 Order 01/61, 12.8.1961, see Riemer, Rudolf, Das zweigeteilte Deutschland 1961–1962, München 1995, P. 119

3 See Beschloss, Michael, Powergame. Kennedy und Chruschtschow. The Crisis Years 1960–1963, Düsseldorf 1991, P. 281

4 Brandt, Willy, Erinnerungen, Berlin³ 1989

5 Edward R. Murrow, see Bechloss, Powergame, P. 279

6 Schlesinger, Klaus, Am Ende der Jugend, in: Der Berliner Traum, Rostock 1977, P. 116f

7 Fundstellen SAPMO-BArch DY 30/IV/2/15287 und Berliner Mauer-Archiv

8 Informationsbericht, Berliner Mauer-Archiv

9 SAPMO-BArch Dy 30 J IV 2/2/2 784

10 Tansportpolizei/Abschnitt Berlin, Berliner Mauer-Archiv

11 See Koop, Volker, Den Gegner vernichten. Die Grenzsicherung der DDR, Bonn 1996, P. 178f

12 de Bruyn, Günter, Vierzig Jahre. Ein Lebensbericht, Frankfurt a.M.² 1996, P. 109f

13 Order 101/69, Cf. Koop, Gegner, P. 260f

14 Order 101/71, Cf. ibid., P. 263f

15 Rundschreiben an SED-Kreisleitungen, 28.10.1971, P. 2 (Berliner Mauer-Archiv)

16 See Scholze, Thomas/Blask, Falk, Halt! Grenzgebiet!, Berlin 1992, P. 183/199

17 LAB, C Rep. 736, Nr. 70; zu Fluchtversuchen Cf. also: Hildebrandt, Rainer, Es geschah an der Mauer, Berlin 1992

18 Orders 101/61 und 101/62, BA-MA VA-01/5003

19 Handbuch für Grenzsoldaten, Berlin 1965, P. 41

20 See Karau, Gisela, Grenzerprotokolle, Frankfurt/M. 1992, P. 25

21 See Koop, Volker, Ausgegrenzt. Der Fall der DDR-Grenztruppen, Berlin 1993, P. 118

22 Vorlage des Stadtkommandanten, Februar 1965 (Berliner Mauer-Archiv)

23 See Knobloch, Heinz u. a., Geisterbahnhöfe, Berlin 1994, P. 77ff

24 See Karau, Grenzerprotokolle, P. 33

25 Cf. Rathje, Wolfgang, Der Ausbau der Berliner Mauer 1975-1989, Mp., Christian-Albrecht-Universität Kiel, 1996, P. 20ff

26 Konzeption ... für den weiteren Ausbau der Staatsgrenze der DDR, 5.8.1982 (Berliner Mauer-Archiv) Cf. dazu Wenzel, Otto, Kriegsbereit: der Nationale Verteidigungsrat der DDR 1960 bis 1989, Köln 1995, P. 71f

28 Schreiben des Grenzkommandos Mitte, Juni 1971, Bl. 1, (Berliner Mauer-Archiv); Politische Verwaltung der Grenztruppen der DDR (Hg.) Die Staatsgrenze unserer Republik ist unantastbar, o.O. 1982, P. 43

29 Übersicht versuchte und erfolgte Grenzdurchbrüche (1.12.1974–30.11.1979) (Berliner Mauer-Archiv)

30 LAB, C Rep. 736, No. 70

31 LAB, C Rep. 736, No. 69

32 See Koop, Ausgegrenzt, P. 114f

33 Handbuch für Grenzsoldaten, P. 55

34 Cf. Geschke, Heinz u. a., Die Sicherung der Staatsgrenze der DDR als gesamtgesellschaftliches System, in: Vom Mauerbau zum Mauerfall, H.5, Potsdam 1998, P. 52

35 Außerordentliche Dienstbesprechung, 23.8.1988, BA-MA GTÜ AZN 16629

36 Schreiben von Oberstleutnant Ganßauge, Oktober 1981, LAB, C Rep. 736, Nr. 12

37 Frankfurter Allgemeine Zeitung, 20.1.1989

38 Kommando der Grenztruppen, „Thesen zum Thema Tendenzen der Entwicklung neuer Grenzsicherungsanlagen...", BA-MA GTÜ AZN 17791

39 See Rathje, Ausbau, P. 143

40 Forschungsbericht „Seismische Meldungsgebersysteme", 31.1.1985, BA-MA GTÜ AZN 17779

41 See Rathje, P. 115

42 Cf. „Vorschlag des Chefs Technik und Bewaffnung der Grenztruppen", 30.12.1988, BA-MA GTÜ AZN 17791

43 Ministerium für Nationale Verteidigung, Juni 1988, BA-MA GTÜ AZN 17791

44 Cf. Hertle, Hans-Hermann, Chronik des Mauerfalls, Berlin 1996, P. 145f

45 Cf. Hertle, Hans-Hermann, Der Fall der Mauer, Opladen 1996, P. 187

46 Neue Berliner Illustrierte 8/1990, P. 4

47 See Hertle, Chronik, P. 14

48 See Hertle, Fall der Mauer, P. 230

49 See Karau, Grenzerprotokolle, P. 21

50 Cf. Hertle, Fall der Mauer, P. 256ff

51 Order 101/89 in der Fassung vom 21.12.1989, BA-MA GTÜ AZN 17239

52 Cf. Grafe, Roman, in: Süddeutsche Zeitung, 3./4.5.1997

Archives used

Bundesarchiv, Außenstelle Dahlwitz-Hoppegarten

Bundesarchiv, Stiftung Archiv der Parteien- und Massenorganisationen der DDR (SAPMO), Berlin

Landesarchiv Berlin

Mauer-Archiv von Hagen Koch, Berlin

Photographes and Documents

Berliner Mauerarchiv 9, 19, 20, 24 (3), 25, 26, 39, 43, 45, 47, 48/49(4), 50, 51, 52, 53, 54, 57, 60 (2), 62, 63

Dieter Breitenborn, Berlin7, 13, 37 (2), 72, 74

Bundesarchiv Koblenz 18

Ch. Links Verlag, Berlin 30, 40, 68, 75

Landesarchiv Berlin 27, 31, 41, 59 (C Rep. 736)

Landesbildstelle Berlin 12, 14, 21, 44

Klaus Lehnartz, Berlin 6, 16, 19 above, 22, 23, 29, 33, 35

Michael Reimer, Berlin 42

Andreas Schoelzel, Berlin 67, 71

UweSteinert, Berlin 76

Ullstein Bilderdienst 17 (Photo: PeterLeibing) 34

Zeitungsarchiv FU Berlin 11

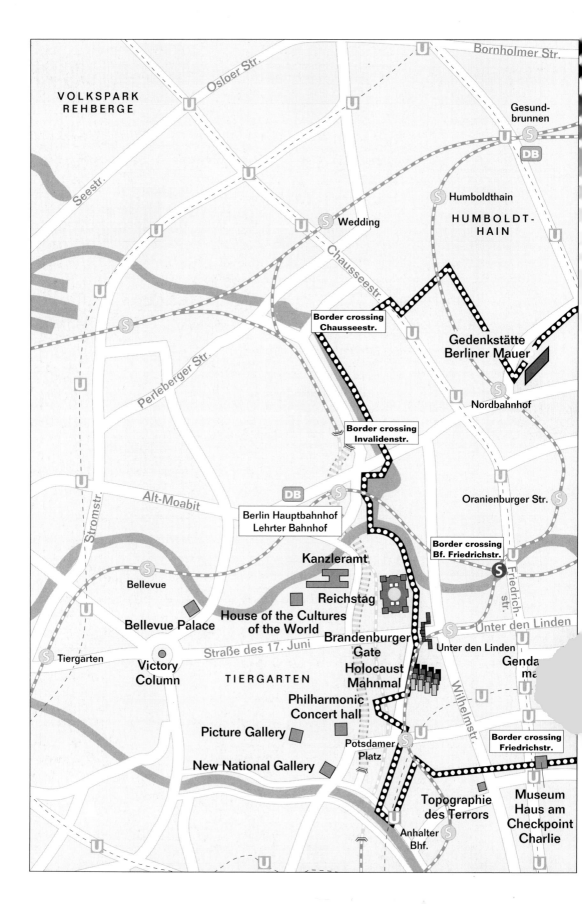